Transforming *Your* LIFE *After* LSS

FINDING YOUR WAY TO PEACE, JOY & HAPPINESS

JOHN CRAFT

ISBN 979-8-9862830-7-4 (paperback)

*This book is dedicated to, and written in honor
of, my parents, Dave & Pauline Craft.*

*I often speak of the critical nature of having a solid foundation.
I wouldn't have won any of my victories nor recovered from
my defeats without that; which they instilled in me.*

*My Mom and Dad made sure I was solid and firm in my
spirit and in my soul. As a result, I was able to step out with
confidence into the world at a younger age than most.*

*Instead of allowing the trials, tribulations, and loss THEY
each experienced at very young ages to break their spirits, or to
define them, they individually built their personal foundations
of wisdom, fortitude, and quiet strength, which is rare.*

*Most would have lived bitter lives. They, instead, intentionally
created lives of tranquility, love and celebration.*

*They transformed THEIR lives and found
peace, joy, and happiness.*

*Thank you, Mom & Dad, from the bottom of my
heart and from the depths of my soul. I love you.*

Contents

Introduction: WHAT YOU CAN EXPECT FROM THE BOOK — 1

Setting the Table: WHAT, WHO & WHY — 5

Secret One: WANTING & WILLING — 17
   WHAT THEY ARE AND WHY THEY'RE IMPORTANT

Secret Two: DECIDE. THEN ACT. — 29

Secret Three: "IT CAN BE LOST" — 35
   UNDERSTANDING, OWNING AND ACCEPTING THOSE WORDS

Secret Four: SURRENDER, BUT NEVER QUIT — 47
   THE OXYMORON EXPLAINED

Secret Five: GRIEF ISN'T A "PROCESS" (PART ONE) — 59

Secret Six: GRIEF CHANGES YOU—SOMETIMES PERMANENTLY — 71

Secret Seven: GRIEF ISN'T A PROCESS (PART TWO) — 77

Secret Eight: GET COMFORTABLE BEING *UN*-COMFORTABLE — 89

Secret Nine: THE POWER OF DISCOVERY — 97

Secret Ten: THE WAY OUT — 109

Secret Eleven: THE ROAD LESS TRAVELED — 121

Secret Twelve: DECIDING WHAT YOU WANT — 129

Secret Thirteen: THE ULTIMATE SECRET — 135
   IT'S *ALWAYS* BEEN UP TO YOU

Your "Next": CREATE A LIFE YOU LOVE — 143

Acknowledgments — 147

About the Author — 153

Thank You Gift!! — 155

WHAT YOU CAN EXPECT FROM THE BOOK

Hey. Good to see you.

I tend to write like I talk and hopefully, I've done that with the book. I want it to read like you and I are sitting together, just having a friendly and compelling conversation.

I've written this book from my soul and from my heart.

A lot of people will think this book is about loss.

And yes, loss is in the title. But the book really isn't about that. Loss is just the catalyst that inspired the book and propelled it into the universe. I'm guessing that loss is the catalyst for you reading it, too.

You may be tired of how your life is today. You may want change. You may *need* change. You may be looking for a way to make that change happen. You may have explored other avenues, looked for other ways to change.

I know I did.

Here's what I'd like you to know: This is what I found. And it works.

The lessons in the chapters ahead stack on top of each other to create a blueprint that you can use to transform your life from what it is today into what you want it to be. To start creating a life you love.

This book isn't theoretical. It's not a philosophy textbook. It's not about a way of thinking. It's much more about a way of being.

This book was born out of my personal experience, my desperate need for change and out of the personal experiences of those I've worked with over the years.

I originally titled the book as "Transforming Your Life After Loss: 13 Secrets Revealed." The reason is that the word "secret" refers to knowledge that is hidden. This knowledge was hidden to me, until I went looking for it.

I uncovered it through an extensive process of research. Of trial and error. Some things I did worked. A lot more didn't.

The knowledge: The concepts and the steps, were slowly revealed to me in a way that made sense, that I could actually use.

And the result of all the trial and error, the work, the frustration and yes, the sleepless nights, is this: I now have a life of hope. One of peace, joy and happiness. A truly transformed life.

This book is the roadmap to that life for you, too.

I want you to know that this thing is as real as it gets. In places, it's a little raw. But loss and grief *are* raw. They're real, and they're no joke.

I experienced major loss in my life. I also experienced all the negative emotions. I experienced overwhelming grief.

But most importantly, I discovered recovery and restoration.

I found my way to peace, joy and happiness. That's what the

book is about. It's a roadmap for you so you can find your own way there.

It's about you finding a way to recover from all of heartache, pain and sadness so you can experience restoration in your life, like I have in mine.

I use the words "the way out" inside the book. But really, the whole book is about a way *in*. It's about finding a way into your transformed, peaceful and restored life.

It can be done. And it's not as hard as some would make it sound. I know. I'm living proof. And I know many others who are also living proof that it's possible to transform your life after loss.

If I can do it and they can do it, guess what?

You can too.

To wrap this up, the book offers 13 secrets to dealing with loss and grief. It's the same roadmap I used to transform my own life from one of pain, chaos, upheaval and turmoil into one of peace, happiness, joy and rest. It's a path, the way out of darkness, back into life and light.

By reading it and applying the lessons contained within, I know you'll be able to transform your life too.

Much love.

John

WHAT, WHO
& WHY

I've taken a very personal journey through loss, and through sadness, loneliness, depression and anger, which are all part of the debilitating grief that comes as a result of loss.

The journey—and I use that phrase because that's what it's been—was not one I bought a ticket for, signed up for, volunteered for, or ever wanted to take.

It was one I was forced into against my will. From 2009 up through the first half of 2020, I experienced many different kinds of loss, and the aftermath. That aftermath got to be very familiar as it seemed to either be the same or have the same components after every loss.

Here's what happened in that eleven and a half year period:

I lost the position I loved, because I was involuntarily transitioned to a different position with the company.

I lost that entire job four years later. (Some people call it being laid-off or downsized.)

I lost my dog to cancer.

I lost my health; I had a massive heart attack and, four years later, underwent treatment for aggressive prostate cancer.

I lost my life during the heart attack; I died in the ER.

I lost my self-confidence.

I lost my Dad.

I lost both of my wife's parents—to cancer.

I lost my wife of 37 years—in less than 3 months—to cancer.

I lost my future.

I lost my reason—and my will—to live.

I lost my purpose.

I lost my drive, my ambition and my desire.

I lost myself.

All of it was personal, and all of it hurt. It felt like both the continuous losing, along with the subsequent pain and grief, would never end. I was always waiting for the other shoe to drop. I had a negative attitude of *"What's next?"* affecting every area of my life.

I wasn't happy or gratified. I was living in a state of constant fear and internal turmoil; of chaos. Outwardly, I looked great. Like I had it all together and had the world by the tail. Inwardly, I was a complete mess. I was dealing with "imposter syndrome"; with guilt; and with stress that would boil over into an external display of anger occasionally. All of it.

However, I'm here today to tell you that cycle *did* stop. Instead of a life of chaos, turmoil and pain, I now live a life of (mostly) peace and joy.

That said, no one can ever get away from loss entirely. It's a part of the human contract. Here's the truth. If you possess or have *ANYTHING,* you can lose it. It can be gone in the blink of an eye, or it can slowly drain away. It can be lost.

Those four small words are powerful: "*. . . it can be lost . . .*"

Understanding and accepting those four words, however, is empowering. This concept alone will strengthen you, allow you to keep moving forward, and is one of the foundational keys to dealing with loss along with its effects and aftermath. It's one of the thirteen secrets and we'll dig into it inside the book.

Moving on, there are probably two types of people who can benefit from this book.

The first type is those who have suffered loss—and are stuck in sadness, pain, despair, the past, grief, or maybe a combination of all of those, and can't seem to be able to get unstuck.

They have, however, decided they want to understand it; are tired of living in the "gray zone;" and believe they are willing to do what it takes to get out.

My heart hurts for you. Because I *was* you. And being stuck in the "gray zone" sucks; it's hard. Heck, *all* of this is hard.

That said, I want you to know there *is* a way out and there is life after loss and grief.

Please note that I didn't say "There can be life after loss and grief." I said "There **IS** life after loss and grief."

That's an important distinction to make, because I'm not talking about just existing, or going through the motions of living; I did that too. I'm talking about really living; about discovering, visioning, creating and experiencing your best life; about creating a life you love living.

There's an expansive, joyous, rewarding life, and a way to really live life on the other side of loss and grief. I know because

I've experienced it, and in fact, *am* experiencing that now. Today, I *am* happy and gratified.

Perhaps this book can help get you on your own road to finding that life. If you want it.

I titled the book "Transforming Your Life After Loss" because it can be done. *You* can do it; you can transform your life. I know—because I have, and if I can do it, anyone can.

The second type of person this book *may* be for is someone who understands that anything or anyone they have can be lost—and wants to get out in front of that in a way that prepares them to deal with it. If that's you, I'm impressed.

Although I will say this as a caveat—and also as fair warning for that type of person. You won't truly or fully understand loss or grief until you experience them both on a deep personal level. Then, perhaps, you'll be able to reference this book as sort of a template for how to navigate it.

I think this is a rare type of person, though. Loss and the associated grief, pain, sadness, despair, depression, anger, etc., which come with it, are not things people often choose to think about or deal with voluntarily. Most people only do so when they're forced into it; when they have no other choice. At least that's how I was.

By the way, if you're reading this book for someone else who has experienced major or traumatic loss, to see if it's "right" for them, please don't.

I'd ask that you let them be the reader. And the judge. You don't know where they're at. You can't. Not until you go through it. So from your perspective, it may not feel right for them, but from their perspective, it may be exactly what they need. Or it may not.

Either way, allow them to make that decision. Thank you.

Here's who this book is NOT for:

There is a point on the Grief Curve™ where people can get stuck. It's called the Pit and it's inside the Danger Zone. These are people who *decide* to get stuck; they make a conscious choice. They stop. They intentionally stop moving forward. They stop trying to help themselves, and/or they stop seeking help. (The Grief Curve™ is fully explained later.)

This book isn't for those people because they're not ready yet. They may be ready at some point in their lives, or they may never be. These are people who want to be victims, who are happy in despair. That may sound like an oxymoron, by the way, but it's not. You and I both know people like this.

People with a victim belief system simply won't get this book; they won't accept it and they won't do the work required to change, because they really don't want to change.

I know. I went through a period—albeit brief—where I thought grief was my friend, and that the Pit was where I should stay in order to be comfortable. Frankly, I was "un-help-able" at that point; in other words, I was stuck. I'd stopped, and I was developing that victim mentality.

I only moved out of it after deciding I wanted to move out of it and then taking action. On some level, I sensed somehow, that there was a way to do it; I just needed to find it. I was lucky. Maybe blessed is a better word.

I discovered people who inspired me and who reminded me of who I really was, so that I could make that decision to move forward.

By the way, grief is not *anyone's* friend, ever. Grief is something else entirely. (More on that later.)

Here's what happened to me as I was moving through all of this.

I did exactly three grief-counseling sessions after my wife died. On the first or second one, the grief counselor, who had lost her husband years earlier, told me that she was there to "witness my pain."

That bothered me. A lot. Because I didn't need a witness; I knew exactly what it felt like and how much it hurt. I needed help to make it NOT hurt so much.

During the third session, because she mentioned her loss again, I found myself beginning to counsel her, so I stopped going. I knew at that point, grief-counseling wasn't going to be right for me. *I* was certainly in no position to try and help her. Now maybe, but not then.

I don't mention this to denigrate her. Not at all. She was doing the best she knew how, and she was putting herself in extremely uncomfortable situations dealing with people like me. I have tons of respect and love for her. The problem was, she hadn't moved past her own grief yet, so consequently I knew she wouldn't be able to help me move past mine.

I also went to exactly two counseling sessions with a psychologist, on the advice of my doctor. This was after Covid had first started, so it was virtual, kind of like a meeting over Zoom.

The first session was basically a "get to know you" meeting, with the doctor asking me questions about what had happened, how I was feeling, how I was sleeping, how I was dealing, etc.

The second session was more of a check-in and check-up. At the end of that one, she said to me, "You're remarkably well-adjusted. There's not anything else I can do for you, so you really don't need to spend any time with me. You just need to go live your life."

I was gratified to hear that, of course. I appreciate & applaud her honesty. But at the same time, when hearing that from her, I did feel like I was kind of all alone out there, navigating this whole journey of loss and grief.

After my wife was gone, I was in a place I'd never been before. And looking back, here's how I processed it. I told myself that I was going to dig into this grief, into this uncomfortableness, and I was going to figure it out—I would seek to first understand it, then seek to mitigate it, to get rid of it.

So, I started analyzing it. I started writing about it and about how I was feeling. I didn't hold anything back; I was screaming onto the page. Sometimes it was just stream-of-consciousness writing; just getting everything out. When I went back and re-read it, it almost didn't make sense . . . but it *did* make sense because it was how I was feeling inside.

During one of my more analytical moments, I came up with what I call the Grief Curve™, which I created to help me visualize what I was dealing with when it came to grief. I also started writing *Grief Killer,* my first book, and one I'll never publish.

And looking back on it, doing all of that stuff—which was not fun, and had more the feel of being on a mission—started to teach me to become comfortable being uncomfortable.

The only way I can write about it, or frankly, even think about it today—is to come from a place of learning to be comfortable being uncomfortable.

Looking back on it now, I can see now that it was literally a life and death lesson for me, and I believe it was partially responsible for me choosing life, for saving me.

Because that realization—learning how to get comfortable being uncomfortable—was what catapulted me forward into the other factors that saved me. (But those are for later.)

I knew that my experience, while certainly not unique, was extremely difficult. I had learned a lot and had experienced a lot of insight while dealing with it, so after 4-plus years of processing it and thinking about it on and off, I decided to write this book.

I've been coaching others in the area of performance for years. I decided to make it official and became a certified life-coach.

I created Craft Method Coaching, LLC, because I think it's important to be available to others to help, as someone who's experienced first-hand what others are going through; to be an objective third party and someone to talk with. And honestly, coaching lights me up inside; it's what I know I was born to do. It's my true calling.

Everything that I talk about and that I teach, I've experienced. I've lived it. Both sides of it. Living it and experiencing it on a very personal level is what makes me an expert. It's not theoretical for me; it's all been very, very real.

Let me wrap this up with what you can expect from this book.

I won't dwell on them, but I will describe and discuss my experiences, and what I went through. This is for two reasons.

One, not because this book is about me. I mean, to some degree, it is, yes, because it's what I lived and learned from, but primarily, I want this book to be not about, but for, *you*.

I want you to truly understand that *I* deeply understand loss, pain and grief on a personal and visceral level. That's important, so you know-that-I-know what you're feeling. I can relate, and since I can relate, perhaps I can help.

That said, however, your journey will look different than mine, because all circumstances of loss are different, for different people.

Two, the lessons I discovered and learned from those experiences are what make up the heart of this book. I've explored them deeply, and I've applied them in my own life. These are pieces of insight, knowledge and tools that you can use and/or adapt, if you so choose, to jump-start you on the way out of a life of pain and grief, into one of rest and peace.

You may not use them like I did. But that won't matter. They're not meant to be "cookie-cutter" tools, nor is this way out of pain a "cookie-cutter" process.

Your path will look different from mine. This *is* a journey. And as with any journey, it's easier with a compass; with a direction. This book can be both your compass and provide you with direction.

Here's what else I know.

When and if you use the thoughts, ideas and tools inside, you'll begin the process of transforming your life from what it is now, into what you want it to be.

But, finally, a word of caution.

This stuff doesn't happen overnight. It takes time, it's messy, and it hurts. I also can't do any of this for you. Frankly, no one can. It's a very personal—and sometimes it can be a very lonely—journey.

I mean, I'd like to be able to do it for you, and I would if I could. It's that important to me . . . I wouldn't wish any of what I felt or what I went through on my worst enemy. I'd like to just wave a magic wand and have it all instantaneously disappear and be replaced with your best life. But I can't.

And maybe it's better that way. Because the process of self-discovery that you'll create and then implement in your life is worth the time, worth the messiness and worth the hurt that you'll go through.

It's worth it all because it'll make you stronger and it'll restore your confidence. Most importantly though, you'll discover what's possible for you.

Instead of believing you'll never get out of it, you'll experience personal *"aha!"* moments, when you see exactly what's next and how to get yourself there.

Fire is a big deal here. Steel is forged and tempered by fire. You are transforming yourself and your life into one of tempered steel.

Through fire, you're re-inventing and re-birthing yourself. The mythical Phoenix is created anew and rises from the ashes; ashes which are created by fire.

This process of recovery and restoration—if you embrace it—will become *your* fire. It's a fire that will forge, temper and create a new you. It's a fire that will create a different you. And a fire that will create a better you.

If you decide to let it. And that's on you.

Please believe that no matter where you are today, that no matter how dark or gray it seems, no matter how much it hurts, no matter how lonely it feels and no matter that you can't see the path ahead, through taking one step at a time, through putting one foot in front of the other, you *can* create a life that you love.

You can break the cycle of pain and grief left in the wake of loss. And you can do it faster than you thought possible. Again, I know.

I remember how endless it felt when I was in it. But I also

remember how quickly it turned around when I got serious about overcoming it—and how surprised I felt at that. I've gone through the fire and come out the other side.

You will too. And while your journey will be different from mine, I'm sure they'll have similarities.

By the way, I'd love to hear your thoughts, insights and questions about the book. I promise you, I'll respond to every well thought out, sincere and honest email.

You can share good stuff with me too, and I encourage you to do so at john@craftmethodcoaching.com.

You can also check out my website at www.craftmethod coaching.com.

Here's my final thought for now:

The first step is the first step.

Here's yours: Turn the page and we'll start with you discovering what wanting and willing are, why they're important, and then go from there.

I'll meet you on the other side.

Much love.

One

Wanting & Willing

What They Are and Why They're Important

This might seem like an odd name for a chapter. But this is the starting place for you to begin transforming your life after loss. Because without it, none of the rest of the information in here will matter. It'll be meaningless. And it won't work.

What do I mean by "wanting and willing?" What am I trying to accomplish by laying these two words out there like this?

Well, the short answer is: nothing.

What?! What do you mean by "nothing," John?

Well, I mean—nothing. Let me explain.

I phrased the question—and the answer—that way for a reason. I phrased both the way I did, because I wanted your mind open and curious when I explained it.

By the way . . . those two things? Being open? And being curious? By themselves, those two attributes are strong. A lot of people—maybe you—are sometimes open, and they're also sometimes curious.

The problem is they're not either all the time. And by "all the time," I mean "most of the time." Pretty tough to be a certain way "all" the time, isn't it? After all, we're people, not robots.

When these two are combined, however—when a person is being both open and being curious—they're more than strong; they're powerful. Very powerful. When someone is both open and curious, it's almost like they have a superpower.

And I'm asking you to be both. To be open. Be curious. Be that way all the way through this book. If you ever feel yourself getting disconnected; or *NOT* being those ways, put the book down. Take a walk. Drink a cup of tea. Or coffee. Focus on consciously being both open and curious. Then come back.

You'll get a lot more out of it. It'll make a much faster, stronger and deeper impact than if you're not.

And those words—"be" or "being"? They're intentional too. Because you and I? We're human "beings," not humans doing. So . . . be.

Back to my explanation of the question "What am I trying to accomplish here?" The answer is: nothing. I'm not trying to accomplish anything.

It doesn't matter where *I'm* trying to go or what I'm trying to do because I've *already* done it, and I *am* doing it every day, in relation to loss, and transforming my own life. That's why I can write the book; it's why I'm qualified. I've done it.

And what matters here is the only thing that matters.

Which is you.

What are **YOU** trying to accomplish? Where do **YOU** want to go? What was the reason **YOU** bought, or were gifted, this book?

You may not know yet. And that's okay. I mean, I would guess that you probably have a big-picture idea of where you want to go with this. Maybe you know what you think you'd like the end result to be. And that's great because that's your starting place.

Or you may *not* have that big-picture idea. You may simply feel lost. You may just be looking for a direction. And that's okay, too. Why? Because that's *your* starting place.

Here's the good news.

Right now, and while we spend time together, it's about **YOU**. I wrote this book for you. I decided to create my company, my podcast, my workshops, keynote speeches and my coaching program for you.

Because I didn't have someone like me when I needed it. I didn't have anybody who had gone through it; who had experienced it; who had consciously torn it all apart and looked at it from every possible angle, then put it back together in a new way.

And I REALLY needed someone like that then. I almost didn't escape the grief vortex. It almost got me. And by "got me," I mean it almost killed me. That may sound dramatic. It wasn't.

But looking back on it, it's frightening how mundane, how small, it actually was. I mean, if something almost kills you (in my mind anyway), I think that thing should be a big scary, hairy monster. But this wasn't. It was all-consuming at the time, true. But it was small. A small, scary, hairy monster. And a more vicious monster never was.

Here's the truth. You can *thrive*, not just survive. We'll discuss that in more detail in *Secret #11*.

For now, I want you to know that you *CAN* transform your life no matter where you're starting from. Whether you have a vision for your life yet or you don't, it doesn't matter.

I want to stop and make a point right now. Want you to get this one down in your soul. Prepare yourself. This one is critically important.

Ready?

Okay.

There is *NO* right or wrong way to transform your life. This is *NOT* a test. Nobody's grading you or judging you. You can't "study" for this; there is no homework. There's only what works for you. And frankly, it's possible that what works for you may not work for somebody else.

When I began this journey in my own life, I could barely see the next minute or the next hour; I certainly couldn't see the next week, month, year, or decade. I *didn't* have a big picture. In fact, I had no picture at all.

As far as I could tell then, all I had was a ruined life. So if you don't have a vision for your life right now, that's OK. And if you do have a big picture, that's OK too. You can start from either place.

And, hey, I may have missed the place that you're starting from entirely. I may not realize, understand, or know where you are right now. There may be some in-between that I'm not thinking of.

But I do know that the reason you've gone this far is this: You want to transform your life.

And there it is. You **want** to.

Wanting and **willing** are about knowing, or deciding, what you **want**, but also being **willing** to have it.

You can't just want it and expect things to change. I want to win the lottery. The fact that I want to hasn't changed my life one iota.

I have to want to win the lottery, then I have to be willing to have what I want.

Why?

Because if someone isn't willing to have what they want, they won't do or be the way they need to do and be in order to get what they want.

Here's how you can test out if what you want is truly what you want:

There are two ways to want something.

The first way, let's call it "A," is to just tell yourself you want it; that's what most people do. Mostly it just ends there. It dies a quiet death, and they never get what they tell themselves they want. This is also where victimhood is born, by the way.

The second way to want something—let's call it "B"—is to want it badly enough to go do something about it. This is the litmus test. When you start doing something about it, you're feeling it on the inside. That means you're willing to have what you want.

When it comes to your transformed life, which one is it for you? A or B?

That's it.

Decide what you want, then be willing to have it. Be able to feel it on the inside and be willing to do something about it, no matter how small or seemingly insignificant.

This is the key. This is the starting point. If you can't or won't do this, then nothing else in here will work for you.

Right now, you may be saying, well of course, John. I know what I want; and if I want something, obviously, I'm willing to have it. I'm going after it. No mountain too high, no ocean too deep, no . . . well, you get the idea.

Really?

You'd think so, wouldn't you?

And in the case of loss, grief, sadness, depression, anger, rage, all of that, you'd think a person would do almost anything to get out of that cycle.

I thought so too.

In my case, because I didn't have a guide like me to cause me to start thinking about this stuff, I *thought* I knew what I wanted, and I *thought* I was willing to have it, but the choices and decisions I kept making didn't align with either one. They weren't helping me get out of the hole I felt like I was in. If anything, it felt like they just kept pushing me deeper.

I mean, I had some crazy ideas, that at the time, felt very rational to me. I'll tell you one.

When I was 17 years old, I enlisted in the United States Marine Corps. I didn't want to go to college, and I wanted to do something to prove myself to myself, to my high school classmates, to my parents and to the world. So, I joined the Marines.

That's the background.

When I was in the radio business, the company I worked for owned radio stations in Butte, Montana. One of the guys that worked there was the brother of Rob O'Neill. Rob is the Navy SEAL who shot Osama Bin Laden, the mastermind behind the worst terrorist attack on the United States in history.

So, Navy SEALS are my personal heroes. As a Marine, it takes a lot to hero-worship anybody else, but SEALS are on a whole different level. You get the picture.

In my isolated, solitary, out-of-my-mind with grief state, I had the brilliant idea that I'd call Rob's brother in Butte, have him connect me with Rob, and finagle a way to go over to Afghanistan and go to war.

I was a peacetime Marine; I served from 1976 to 1980, so my twisted logic told me this was my chance to saddle up, train hard for 13 weeks, get back in shape, and then go run through the desert as a military contractor, searching for and killing terrorists.

My mind literally told me that this was a good idea. It was telling me this was what I wanted. That this was the way to get all of the rage, the anger and the sadness out of me. I mean, I was completely convinced. Or so I told myself.

But let's dive a little deeper. I can do this now, with hindsight as my guide. Couldn't do it then, though.

I shared this with my daughter, with my mother and with a friend. My daughter and my friend both told me I was crazy, without saying I was crazy. But that's what they meant.

My Mom is a rockstar. She didn't react at all. She just looked at me, and asked me, *"John, do you want to do something to hurt yourself?"*

Talk about cutting to the chase! And the way she asked wasn't accusatory. It was an honest and genuine question. She was being both open, by asking what was on her mind, and being curious because she truly wanted to know if that was what I wanted.

Which started me thinking. Because on some level I hadn't admitted to myself yet, I knew this was a stupid idea. So *did* I want to cause harm to myself? Was that what was driving these obviously crazy thoughts? Was that what I really wanted?

So, I thought about it some more. Her questions got the wheels turning in a different direction. I started drilling down into what I really wanted.

And what I decided was that no, I didn't want to hurt myself.

What I really wanted was to put passion and excitement and color back in my life.

I was tired of living in a gray world. I was tired of not having the desire to do anything except get up, feel miserable, cry my eyes out, get drunk, rage at the universe, then go to sleep, wake up exhausted and start the cycle all over again.

Because, sometimes, knowing or deciding what you *don't* want, is just as important as deciding what you *do* want.

It was for me.

Because of an insightful question from my mother, I had backed into and discovered and decided what I really did want. And I also decided that yes, I was willing to have it. I felt it on the inside, and it felt good. I was willing to do something about it.

That other thing? What it made me feel was nervous and uncertain. That's because it was a false want.

So put *your* want to the test. Is it A or B for you? Does your want make you feel good on the inside? Or does it make you feel the opposite of good?

We're going to talk a bit more about you discovering, deciding, then knowing what it is you want.

But let's really simplify it. Let's boil it down to what you want your transformed life to look like. After all, the name of the book is *Transforming Your Life After Loss*.

That must resonate with you somehow, or you wouldn't still be reading. What does that mean to you? For you? What do you *WANT* your transformed life to be? What do you *WANT* it to look like? How does it make you feel on the inside?

Right now, just describing those two things in a very general way is fine. You can drill down into details later. The point is, that right now, I simply want you to discover, decide and then know, in an "I-know-that-I-know-that-I-know" feel-good kind of way inside you of what that is.

So when you finish this chapter, I want you to do one thing.

Get a piece of paper, or do it on your computer. Don't do it on your phone.

Write down what YOUR transformed life looks like. Pretend you have it now. And answer these two questions:

One, what is it?

Two, what does it look like?

That's your starting point. Because we're not going to focus on all the crap you're dealing with and going through now. You know what that is already. We don't need to describe it or dwell on it or wallow in it. Hey, you're living it. You know what "now" is like.

I want you to shift; to focus on your transformed life. Not on your now, but on your "next." You need to begin to get a picture of what your transformed life is, what it looks like and what it feels like to live it. This is another secret besides the 13 in this book. This is how you start creating your transformed life.

Answer these two questions and write them down. Be as detailed or as simple as you want to be. Remember: no right, no wrong.

There's just what is. There's your "next."

That's it for this chapter.

Get to it. I'll see you when you turn the page.

Two

Decide.
Then Act.

Hey. Good to see you. I mean that sincerely, by the way. It *IS* good to see you. Perhaps not everybody has turned the page; perhaps not everyone will have written down what they want their transformed life to look like.

We may have scraped a few people off from the end of the last chapter to the beginning of this one.

And that's okay.

Remember . . . I said earlier that there's no judgment, no grade, no right, no wrong here. There's just what is.

But since you're here?

You've already done what the title of this chapter is. You've decided. And you've acted.

You have decided that you want to transform your life into what you want it to be, rather than what it is now. You're fed up with your "now" and you're ready for your "next."

So, you're acting.

The verb "to act" is not passive. Is it descriptive? Yes. Is it also a defining word? I believe it is. But it is also something you do.

Remember the two ways to want something? If you don't, take a moment, go back and find that passage in the last chapter and read it again, then come back here.

This is your "B," the second way to want something. You want it badly enough to go and do something about it. This is the litmus test. When you start doing something about it—and you are—that means you're willing to have what you want.

The next step, knowing—or in this case deciding—what you want, then being willing to have it is one act, or action. The next action is following through and continuing.

You're willing, and you're demonstrating that willingness, you're giving it life, you're doing something about it, no matter how small or seemingly insignificant. And continuing on with this book may appear small.

It is not small, however.

It. Is. *HUGE!!!*

Because it's the key. It's your starting point. You have decided what you want, and by deciding that, you've also decided what you don't want, what you won't accept anymore, and that's just as important. Knowing or deciding what you won't accept, is just as important as deciding what you will.

This is how you focus on your transformed life. Not by seeing your "now," but by seeing your "next."

This is a very short chapter, for a reason.

We don't need to dwell on this. You get it, but I still wanted to emphasize it. Because it *deserves* its own chapter.

You've decided. And you've acted. But let's not keep it past tense.

Let's make it present tense, and let's keep it that way. Not only have you acted, but you are acting, and you will continue to decide and to act (future-tense). You've decided and are predicting your future action.

There's a structure to this book, to the way it's written and how it's laid out. The way the secrets are ordered and presented is intentional.

It's "stackable." Every new concept is meant to stack on top of the last one. *Secret #2* is meant to stack on top of *Secret #1*; *Secret #3* on top of *Secret #2*, and so on.

But not in a way that obliterates the Secret that it stacks on top of. You're building a foundation. The tallest buildings in the world have the largest and strongest foundations. They couldn't be skyscrapers if they didn't. The wind, storms and elements would knock them down.

In the same way, your life can't be a "skyscraper" without a strong, deep and large foundation, either. The storms of life will knock you down, they'll crush you if you don't. They'll obliterate you.

The first five chapters, starting with "Who, What & Why" up through *Secret #4*, are foundational chapters. They create the base for the next three chapters, which are explanatory chapters. These first eight chapters combined and stacked on top of each other in this order, then create the foundation for the final six chapters, for the "doing" part.

Yes. We could skip right to the "doing" chapters. Then this book would be even shorter.

But without the foundational and explanatory base, nobody would "do the things." Or if they did, it would be just going through the motions, with no passion, no belief and no commitment behind them. "The things" wouldn't be effective. They wouldn't work. And this would all be a waste of your time and money.

So do the work. *(You are.)* Put your hardhat on. Zip up your orange vest. I can hear the beeping of the cement trucks as they back up to the worksite of your life and begin to pour the concrete of your foundation.

Can you hear them?

The explanatory chapters allow the concrete to cure, to get rock-hard and become established in your mind.

Everything is created twice. First in your mind, in your imagination and your vision, and only then can they be created in your reality.

This creation process is where the passion, belief, excitement and the commitment for you to transform your life into one you'd love living comes from. It's where they're poured into your foundation.

That's when you're ready to start construction; to build the skyscraper of your transformed life that *CAN'T* be bent, broken, twisted, shattered or obliterated, no matter what comes against it, no matter what storms life throws at you.

You'll have built a life of bricks, not of straw.

Got it?

Okay. No homework in this chapter. Let's move onto the next foundational piece called *"It Can Be Lost."*

I'll meet you there.

"It Can Be Lost"

Understanding, Owning and Accepting Those Words

Alright. We're going to start digging deeper. Since you've come this far, you're ready.

But be warned. Please.

This will be a difficult chapter for you. In some ways, it might be the most difficult one in the entire book.

But I'll make you a promise. This is also a "breakthrough" chapter. Meaning that if you hang in there, if you *DO* what I'll be asking you to do (*and yes, there's some doing involved*), you'll make headway that very few ever make.

This chapter, combined with the next one (which is the final "foundational" chapter), will set you up for rapid, unprecedented and amazing success. Success you never saw coming.

But they're just the set-up; just the beginning. You'll have set your bar high, but because you'll have these five chapters under your belt and in your toolbox, you'll also be able to clear your bar with ease, then raise it even higher, clear it again, and on and on.

Stackable growth.

As a result of stackable learning.

Hmmm . . . must be some kind of correlation here.

Remember when I said that after you lay your strong foundation, you'll be ready to start building the skyscraper of your transformed life?

One that *CAN'T* be bent, broken, twisted, shattered, or obliterated, no matter what comes against it, no matter what storms life throws at you?

This chapter, depending on what you do with it, will strengthen that foundation. When a foundation is poured, the cement is goopy, soupy, and wet. And it's poured over what's called re-bar. These are steel rods interlaced through the entire foundation area, so that as the cement sits and hardens, it fastens around a steel core, making it stronger.

You can't see the process taking place. About the only noticeable change is the cement changes from goopy to hard and the color changes slightly. That's all you can see from the outside.

But, the real transformation has taken place inside the foundation where it can't be seen. That cement has become concrete. That concrete has a core of hardened steel running all through itself. The cement has accepted the re-bar and gotten much stronger as a result. It's been transformed.

I want you to remember that point about accepting. We'll get to it in a minute.

Guess what? That's a word-picture of you. The point is, there may be slight external changes, such as you frowning less and smiling more, or something like that, but the REAL change will occur inside of you and this chapter helps you acquire the steel core you need.

But, it's a tough one. Like steel, it's hard.

Because we have to talk about the elephant in the room.

About the 800-pound gorilla unblinkingly staring at you from across the table.

And that means we have to talk about loss. Very directly.

I try very hard not to lecture in this book, but instead get you to understand, own and accept the thoughts, and techniques in here.

Well, I'm going to break my own rule here. This is such an important step, that I feel I must reinforce it with strength. Because if you blow by it, or gloss over it, or simply refuse to do it, there will be a consequence. And probably one you don't want.

You won't be able to create the transformed life that I know you want.

Because as hard as this chapter may be to read and—even harder—to do what it talks about doing, once you do it? Once you understand, own and accept that you can lose whatever and whoever you have?

It's freedom. You'll break chains you didn't even know were encircling you. And believe me—they're there.

I hear 'em clanking.

The reason freedom is here is because you'll have the tools you need in order to deal with any loss you ever experience ever again in your life.

People are afraid of the unknown. That's what creates fear. Think about it for a minute. Think about the last time you felt fear—of any kind. It was because you didn't know what was going to happen next.

That's why people fear loss. It's why I did. It's why people fear and why—most of them anyway—hate change. They don't know what's going to happen next. I could go on and on.

I'm not going to sugarcoat this or mince words here. I'm going to come out and say what's necessary.

Here's the lecture part. But it's a short lecture. It's the next two sentences:

This is non-negotiable. You can't transform your life after loss without doing what the chapter title states.

You *MUST* understand, own and then finally accept that everything, anything and anyone you have now *can be lost.*

It can be lost.

Lecture over. I guess it was four sentences.

There are simply no guarantees that anything will stay around forever. And if you're reading this, you know that for a fact, for a truth, albeit a hard truth, because you've experienced it.

Or are experiencing it.

You know that who or what you have can be lost.

Lost forever.

Irredeemably.

Meaning you can never get them, or it, back.

That's exactly what happened to me. I watched it happen. And I was helpless to stop it.

That may have also happened to you. If so, let me just say I'm sorry.

I hurt for you. But I also know this.

In order to get to your transformed life, to your "next," you simply must understand this truth. It's impossible to move on, impossible to start transforming your life until you get this on a gut level.

The second step is to own that truth. To make it personal. To know that it isn't just a random concept, it's a hard truth that applies to you.

Then the final step after you both understand and own it is to accept it.

Remember how the rebar accepts the cement? And after it does and cures, how it's transformed into concrete? That's what you have to do to create transformation. Accept.

Accepting it also means opening yourself up to the pain of the loss. To the hurt. To the anger. To the sadness. To the rage. To the depression. To the . . . *(you can fill in the blank)* . . . with whatever it is that you're feeling.

To *ALL* of it. And this is where it gets hard.

Because I know that, up until now, you've been doing everything you can to push that pain, that hurt and all of those other feelings away or down. To suppress them.

Sure, you might let them in—partially—for a few minutes, but it's always an ongoing and active exercise to push through them, to—as they say—"carry on," to have a "stiff upper lip" and all that garbage.

And it *IS* garbage. Because there *is* no "carrying on" or having a "stiff upper lip" after you suffer a traumatic loss. There just isn't.

You might fool others temporarily because they're not around you all the time and you can put up a good front, but this just doesn't exist. Not unless you're a psychopath or sociopath—which means you have no emotions.

I'm a tough dude. I'm tough mentally and emotionally. I thought I could manage my emotions. Ask me about my "David" story sometime.

And my loss was one that I really fought, that I struggled with. It was hard for me; and it felt impossible. It allowed me to discover that I wasn't as strong as I thought I was.

It caused me to second-guess myself like crazy; to play the what-if game; to be consumed by guilt; to lay awake night after night asking, "what did I do wrong" and "what didn't I do that I should have done" over and over. It caused me to beat the hell out of myself and was eating me alive.

There *was* no "carrying on." For me. And if somebody had told me that? I bet you can guess what the outcome of that little interaction might have been.

Because for me, there was just one moment to the next. Literally.

Perhaps you can relate.

Back to emotions. If you're reading this, you DO have emotions and feelings. You're feeling them now. You're also suppressing them now. Right this very minute.

Aren't you?

And if you answered "no" to that question, I'm going to give you a little tough love right now, call you out and say that you're lying. To yourself.

Second lecture: Telling yourself that you're not suppressing or fighting your emotions is a defense mechanism. You believe that you're protecting yourself from hurt, from pain. But that's not true. You're actually increasing the impact the pain has on you.

Pushing those feelings away, suppressing them, letting them in partially, then slamming the "feelings" door, is exhausting. Because to feel them is to feel hurt, to feel pain. You know it'll hurt, so it goes back to being willing. Are you willing to let the pain in, to feel it fully in order to defeat it?

I know.

That's what I did. I fought the feelings, instead of letting them in; instead of feeling them fully and accepting them.

I had an epiphany which gave me a way to deal with these emotions. Maybe it'll help you too.

I would be sitting there and suddenly, without any warning, a wave of grief would start to wash over me. I could be anywhere, doing anything; it didn't matter.

When it hit me, it was like a tsunami. I'd go from zero to sixty on the grief scale, meaning that one second, I was dry-eyed, not feeling much, then *WHAM!!* I was sobbing, fighting so hard to **NOT** feel the pain, yelling at it and the universe . . . all of it. It lasted until I was worn out. I remember driving down the road just bawling uncontrollably and barely being able to see through the tears. It was *weird*, because this happened over and over and it came out of the blue!

Three years later, one of my coaches, Jason Su, taught me that emotions *DO* come in waves. So, the tsunami analogy is pretty close to right on. Typically, emotions build, crest, then they recede. He also taught me a specific technique for dealing with these emotions that didn't wear me out. He taught me to quit trying to manage them; that it was a zero-sum game and one I'd always lose. Instead, he taught me how to accept them.

The emotions still come once in a while, you know. They still show up. Something will trigger them. Not as often, certainly, but when they do come, I consciously let them all the way in and practice the technique I'll teach you later to deal with them.

And I come out the other side feeling refreshed and relieved, instead of feeling sad and exhausted. I'm bright-eyed, even if I've shed a tear or few. Excited about my future instead of depressed about my past and present. Feeling good, as opposed to feeling sad, depressed or guilty. Or any one of a thousand other bad feelings.

The secret to handling my emotions is that first, I must willingly and fully let them in. All the way in. Meaning I have to allow myself to be open and to be curious (remember those?), and know that I'm going to feel all the sadness, pain, hurt, anger, rage, whatever is. I have to allow the feelings to exist inside of me.

I have to *accept* them.

What makes this easier though, is I also realize that like a wave, they'll crest, but only so high and they they'll recede. I just have to be patient and be willing to let them run their course. That gives them limited power over me.

The feelings aren't *not* going to exist. They were there. They can come back.

When I suppressed my feelings, they were lurking, just waiting to ambush me like I described above. This happened countless times. It exhausted me. It wore me down and wore me out.

That was really the impetus for me to start digging into them, to try and understand it. That's when I wrote "Grief Killer" and when I developed the "Grief Curve™."

But I didn't have this tool. I didn't have a methodology to work with them. I didn't realize that I had to understand, own, and accept them.

Let's circle back. I had to understand, own, and accept that everything else I had and all the other people in my life could all be lost too.

I fought that.

Until I didn't.

I'm not sure what else I can say about this.

Except this: Because you want to move to the next step of transforming your life, you need to feel all of your feelings. All the way.

Here's a technique you can use.

The next time you start to feel any emotion—sadness, anger, grief, even joy or happiness—don't suppress or fight it. Sit down, close your eyes and consciously let it all the way in. See it in your mind as a wave.

See it begin to build as it moves toward you. Then watch it crest and feel it crash onto you. That's when the emotion is the most intense, right there as it covers and engulfs you. After that, you'll notice it recede and the intensity diminishes, until the ocean of your emotion is calm once again. You're not fighting it.

What you're doing is *experiencing* it instead. And by letting yourself experience it, you've begun the process of accepting it. You understand how it works and by letting it in, you're owning it. That allows you to accept it.

Emotions are waves. They build, crest, and recede.

Understand this. Own it. Accept it. Consciously practice this over and over; every time one comes.

Then you'll be ready for the final foundational chapter: *"Surrender; But Never Quit."*

That's next. See you in there.

Surrender, But Never Quit

The Oxymoron Explained

Hey, glad you're here.

So, did you do it? Remember at the end the last chapter, we talked about what to do when you felt an emotion? Any emotion. Did you use the technique?

When you started to feel an emotion, did you sit down, close your eyes, and consciously let it all the way in? Did you see it as a wave in your mind?

Did you see it start to build and move toward you? Did you watch it crest and feel it crash onto you, covering and engulfing you? Did you see it recede, to diminish until the ocean of your emotion was calm again?

Instead of fighting it, did you allow yourself to experience it? Do you now understand that by experiencing it, you've begun the process of accepting it?

Does it make sense to you that emotions are waves? That they build, crest and they recede?

By understanding this, owning and accepting it, you've limited the power these emotions have over you. They're limited because you understand what they really are and how they act. They can only have so much impact. Interestingly, I discovered their impact decreasing every time I employed this technique.

You can do so much too. So much *more!* Are you realizing yet that it's not about you controlling your emotions? And really, that it never has been? You can't control your emotions. They're going to come whether you want them to or not. This is about you being willing to experience them, to feel them, and feel them all the way through. Build, crest, recede. That's all they can do. Nothing more.

Sounds and seems a little counter-intuitive, doesn't it? But it's the answer. It works.

It's real progress.

If you don't quite get it yet, don't worry. You will. By practicing this over and over, every time an emotion shows up—you will.

And that's a great segue into the topic of this chapter. It's called *"Surrender—But Never Quit—The Oxymoron Explained."*

There's a difference between the two, you know. And you might think I'm splitting hairs, or that it's a fine line—and it may be.

But that doesn't change the fact that the line is there. And this is the oxymoron. The difference between surrendering and not quitting.

Here's what happened to me. Let me tell this story, and maybe it'll help you understand what I mean. I call it "stopping."

➢ STOPPING

After my wife died, from what was a brutal and exhausting 14-week and two-day battle, I was completely lost. I was rudderless. I didn't know what I was supposed to do.

I knew what I was supposed to do when she was going through it. When I was her caregiver, I had a mission. I had a job to do. But when she died that suddenly stopped. And I mean, BOOM! No more mission. No more job.

What now?

I tried working. That didn't work. I tried drinking. That didn't work. I tried to re-organize my life into segments, into blocks, into achieving things I hadn't had a chance to pursue. That didn't work either.

I tried listening to music, turned up loud. Nope. That didn't work. I tried watching movies and tv series I'd loved. No interest. That didn't work.

Nothing worked.

I remember waking up one day, and just not wanting to do anything. I had no interest in doing a thing. And I don't mean the kind of "I'm bored" feeling we all experience occasionally . . . I mean I had NO INTEREST. In. Any. Thing.

For example . . . I love to cook and to eat. Food had no flavor and I wasn't hungry.

I love to play poker. I had zero desire to go do that.

I love to read. Couldn't stay focused.

I love to watch good movies and tv series—the well written ones with an awesome and twisty story . . . because I love the art of story. No go.

This was such a different feeling than anything I'd ever experienced before that it got my attention. It piqued my curiosity. It felt like I was moving through molasses, that the world had lost all of its color, and it was just a gray, drab planet I had no place in, nor did I feel any excitement about anything on it.

I had never, ever, felt that way before. I also felt like it should scare me, but since I had no interest in anything, I didn't even feel scared. I just didn't care. This was beyond apathy.

I wondered if this was a prelude to becoming suicidal, to thinking about taking my own life, so I could be with her. And I determined it wasn't that. I knew because I had no interest in that at all.

So, some part of my mind began to analyze it. To try and figure out what it was, and what was happening. Because I knew it was "something" and probably something big. But I didn't know what it was. I simply could not explain or process it.

Eventually, I realized I was at the point of simply stopping. Of giving up. Of quitting.

I don't really know how to even explain it. Because I would never do anything to intentionally harm myself; I just wasn't in that head space. Like I said, I had no interest in that.

But I felt like I could just sit there in my chair in the living room, and just stop. Quit. And whatever happened after that would be fine. If I lived, okay. If I died, okay. I had no interest one way or the other. And it was different from telling myself I didn't care. I simply had no interest. It's the only way I can begin to explain it. It was weird.

And while that realization didn't scare me (remember, I had no passion), it *DID* make me start to think.

➢ Accept the Help You Find

I *wasn't* a quitter. I *wasn't* a "giver-upper." That wasn't me. Never had been, never would be, I told myself. I also felt—and do feel—strongly about things. I had, and I have today, lots of different interests. I'm a naturally curious person.

So I started Googling things like "never quit," "don't give up," etc. And what came up that really caught my eye was Marcus Lutrell's "Never Quit" Foundation. For those of you who don't know, Marcus Lutrell is a former Navy SEAL who wrote the book *"Lone Survivor"* which was also adapted into a movie of the same name.

The point of the title of both the book and the movie, is that Marcus Lutrell WAS the Lone Survivor of that mission. His entire SEAL team was killed in combat.

He barely made it out, but he did more than survive. He didn't quit. He lived the SEAL creed. I won't quote the whole thing here, you can research it on your own if you're interested, but the beginning and end are for me, the most important pieces of it.

It starts with "I will never quit. I persevere."

And it ends with "I am never out of the fight."

He got my attention. Through this, I was reminded of who and what I am. I fell back on the fact that I was a United States Marine. At any given point in time, U.S. Marines make up roughly .006% of the entire US population. If my math is right, that's six-hundredths of one percent.

That means I'm a part of a *VERY* small club. I'm elite, and

I'm in elite company. I'm special. I did what 99.994 percent of the population can't do.

And that's something. My chest is swelling a little bit with pride right now as I write this. Because WE—the Marines—we have our motto too: *"Once a Marine, ALWAYS a Marine."* A Marine isn't something we do; it's something we earn and something we become. It's how we live. It's who we are. Ask any Marine.

Most importantly, I'm a warrior. I'm a fighter. I will never quit. I persevere. I will never give up. Ever! No matter what the fight. No matter the odds. No matter how strong, how mean, how overpowering or how determined the enemy is, I will never quit.

Except I almost did. And THAT finally scared me.

At the beginning of this book I went through the laundry list of everything I've lost. And the biggest was that I'd lost myself. But when I found Marcus and his foundation, and I saw that creed, it was like blinders fell off my eyes and I could see who I was again. The Bible talks about the "scales" falling away from someone's eyes, so they could see. That's exactly what it felt like.

I was no longer stopping, and I wasn't quitting. I was moving ahead under my own power. I wasn't full steam ahead yet, but I could feel myself gaining momentum.

Because I made the words "Never Quit" my motto. Because THAT—those two words—**<u>NEVER QUIT</u>**? That resonated in my soul! That got me back into life.

Was it easy? Not even close. Was it instantaneous? No. It was a process. And I bought a bunch of The Never Quit Foundations black rubber bracelets that say *"Never Quit."* I always wear one and I give them away.

That Never Quit mindset . . . no, it's more than a mindset. It's a way of life, of being. I grabbed onto that like a drowning man would a life jacket. I needed that. I needed to "Never Quit." And I didn't. I pushed through. One baby step at a time maybe, but I did.

That's part of my story. And it's about the quitting part, or maybe a better way to say this, is that it's about the Never Quitting part. I almost did; I came within inches of the precipice, but I didn't. I persevered. I wasn't out of the fight.

And I would like for you to adopt that as your motto as well. Never Quit. Because it'll get you through some rough seas; some tough times.

But now, let's talk about what surrendering is. Because in this context, it's different. This surrendering isn't the type of surrendering a losing army does on a battlefield.

You may not know this about me, but I'm a believer in and follower of Jesus Christ. I know He has my back, and He has my life in the palm of His hand. He literally brought me back from the dead when my heart stopped beating. Through His direction, I was in the exact place I needed to be at the exact right time I needed to be there, or I wouldn't be here today. That was back in 2011. I've seen His work in my life and the life of my family and friends my entire life.

Please, please, *please* don't let my beliefs push you away, or take you out of the book here. Listen. Read this next part. Even if you're not a believer. Because this is real, man. It happened. And it happened to me. I'm living proof, and I'm right here for you to see.

Here's what I did, and here's why that context in the previous two paragraphs is important.

I surrendered. To Him. I didn't give up. I didn't quit. I just surrendered. Here's what I mean, and how I did it.

I was so tired of not being interested in anything. I was exhausted. I felt like there was no color in my life or the world. It all felt gray, and drab and I felt like I was living in a molasses jar. Everything seemed so sticky, so slow. I had no interest, no excitement, and no passion for anything. Or for anybody. I wasn't reaching out. I wasn't communicating. I wasn't doing anything. I was only existing.

So, I prayed. And by the way, I believe He gave me the words, because they certainly didn't come from my heartbroken mind at the time.

I prayed these words: "Dear Lord, please put color, passion and excitement back into my life. In Jesus' name, Amen."

That was it. That was how I surrendered. That was all I knew to do. And then I waited. I went to bed that night and woke up the next morning fully expecting to feel excited about something; to see things differently.

I wasn't and I didn't. I still felt the same.

Same for the next day.

But something had subtly shifted. I didn't recognize it then at all, and it's hard to see it now. But I do see it. What had changed were two things. One, I had decided to Never Quit, and that was my bedrock; that was the hill I'd planted my flag on. Two, was that I had something outside of myself to focus on. I was looking for and expecting the world to get colorful again, to feel excited and passionate about something. I was looking for that and expecting it.

By the way, He answered that prayer. He did it in a way that I never saw coming. It's pretty cool. It ALL happened. God DOES have a sense of humor. I'll talk about it later in the book in *Secret #11* when I cover restoration.

But it all started with surrendering. To this day, I'm still not sure how I came to that conclusion. In fact, I'm not sure that I came up with it at all. I think Jesus did.

I think He knew that I had to realize that I couldn't control any of this. And as a Type-A personality, I had a need to control things. Remember, I also didn't have the tools I have today to deal with emotions.

The only "tool" I had was my belief in God and that Jesus was with me always and through all of this. So I used it. I surrendered it all to Him. I let go. I literally cast my life on Him. I gave it to Him. And my attitude was whatever happened after that, happened.

I understood it, I owned it and I accepted it.

Why? Because I just couldn't do it anymore. It was too big for me. It was simply too much, and I was too tired, too worn out. I had no gas left in my tank. I was so exhausted physically, mentally and emotionally. Every way a person can be exhausted, that was me.

Wow. Looking back on it now, remembering the experience, and then cataloging everything that's happened since. It's nothing short of miraculous. It almost gives me chills. It DOES give me chills!

My life has been completely transformed after major loss.

That's the difference—at least it's MY difference—between surrendering and quitting/ giving up. They are different.

And surrendering saved my life. Again.

No homework this time.

When you're ready, turn the page and we'll get into the next three chapters where we discuss grief.

See you in there.

SECRET

Five

Grief Isn't a "Process"

Part One

My life has been completely transformed after major loss.

And yours can be as well.

It's because of all this that I'm writing this book. All of it works together, you see. One piece by itself is meaningless. And not transformative at all. Surrendering saved my life. Because I was still alive, I was able to put all of the rest of this together. Surrendering was one piece, one part.

But the sum is greater than its parts. Meaning that by themselves, any one or two pieces don't really mean anything. But when you put them all together, it's explosive.

That's the power behind all of this.

And for us to continue to move forward through the process, we have to talk about, understand and deal with grief. I have so much to say about it, that I'm devoting three chapters to it.

We have to define what grief is.

We have to learn how to kill it and get it out of our lives, not cope with it or learn how to live with it.

Let's start with what it *isn't*.

Grief isn't a "process." It doesn't come in "stages." It's not something you can "cope" with. It's not a state of mental health. And time certainly does *not* heal all wounds.

Now before every psychologist, psychiatrist counselor out there gets upset with me over this statement, let me be clear.

Grief isn't an absolute state of mental health. But it can, and often does, affect mental health significantly. And I'm not saying there's not a time and place to seek health from a mental-health professional. That depends on the individual and is that person's decision to make, not mine.

That said, however, let me also be clear about this. What makes people experts on grief, isn't education. It's not training nor is it a title. You become an expert on grief in only one way— by being thrown into it and being forced to live with it.

So I'm an expert on grief. And if the severity of the grief that I dealt with was a degree, I'd have a PhD. What makes me an expert is simple. I went through it. I dealt with it. And I conquered it.

When you Google "stages of grief" there are either five or seven stages of grief depending on your outlook and the seven are simply an expansion of the five. You also learn they have an order. The five stages of grief as defined by Google are: denial, anger, bargaining, depression and acceptance.

This certainly was not my experience. There was no "order" to the grief I dealt with. I never had any denial that she had died; that was reality. I was there when it happened, and I saw it. I sure didn't expect her to come around the corner at any minute.

I didn't do any bargaining, either. I mean, what the heck would I bargain for? She was gone.

My experience of grief was that it was complete and utter chaos. It was overwhelming. Maybe that's why humans created these stages. They wanted try and give order to something that defies order. It's a coping mechanism perhaps, and from my experience a poor one. It didn't work for me.

I had two interactions with mental health professionals during this process. The first was with a grief-counselor who worked for the hospice provider that had taken care of my wife. I had three sessions of grief-counseling with that counselor. And I have a ton of respect for that woman. She had a very difficult job to do and a very difficult person to deal with—me.

But in the very first session, she looked at me and said, *"I'm here to be a witness to your pain."*

Huh? A what? A witness to my pain? I didn't need a witness to my pain! I knew how much it hurt. I knew how strong it was. I was living with it every second of every day. What I needed was someone who knew how to get rid of that pain. I also found out that her husband had died several years prior, and to me, it felt like she was still stuck in that place; stuck in her own grief.

As I determined later, when I developed the Grief Curve™, people CAN get stuck at the bottom of it. I'll touch on it and show it later.

After the third session, when I felt like I was finding myself trying to console her, I determined that I was done. One, I was in absolutely no place to try and help someone else through this. I didn't know enough yet. And two, this wasn't how or where I wanted or needed to spend my limited energy and infinite time. So I never went back. I also asked the hospice provider to take me off their mailing list. They did an okay job, but I didn't want the reminders in the mail of what had happened.

My second interaction with a mental health professional took the form of two virtual visits with a psychologist. It was on the advice of my doctor right after the pandemic had started and all the lockdowns had begun.

She was great. She was very smart and very nice, and she asked good questions. I could tell she was outstanding in her profession. She gave me some great advice on sleeping better. At the conclusion of our second visit, she told me that I was remarkably well-adjusted, and I didn't need to see her again, unless there was something I felt like I wanted to talk about.

I thanked her, told her I'd reach out if I did, and that was that. I haven't seen anyone since.

But I wanted to understand this grief I was feeling.

➤ Grief Is a Monster; It Wants to Kill You

Here's how I define grief. First, grief is created because of loss; it's a by-product of it. Without loss, you won't experience grief. So, understand that grief, even though it feels like the end of the world, just isn't that big. It's a by-product. It's secondary. The loss is the biggie here.

Here's an excerpt from another book I was writing at the time called *Grief Killer*. It's how I view grief:

"Grief is a monster. Plain and simple. It wants to devour you. At best, it wants to chew you up and spit you out, so that there's nothing left of the original you, you're just a husk, a shell of your former self. No light, no life, no love and no joy in you. None.

At worst, it wants to utterly destroy you. To annihilate you in all ways; spiritually, emotionally, mentally and physically.

It wants to literally kill you; it wants you to die.

Among other things, grief is an evil spirit and it's a selfish emotion—all wrapped up into one."

In short, grief is your enemy. It was certainly mine. Here's what I found about defeating enemies. I think it's my interpretation of one of Sun Tzu's precepts from his book *The Art of War.* Wherever it came from, it's wisdom.

To defeat our enemy, we must first understand him. We must know his motivations; we must evaluate his tactics and his strategies. We must learn to recognize his attack triggers. We must understand what his end-game is, and we must understand what his ultimate goals are, for both him and us.

To defeat him, we must develop counterstrategies and tactics of our own. The difference, and the art of it, is that our strategies and tactics must be at a much higher level than his; thereby initially minimizing him. This approach (which is a strategy in and of itself), gives us both time and space (breathing room), to employ those same tactics.

Allow me to address a few things that may have caught your attention.

"Grief is a monster; it wants to kill you." Understand that one. It wants to kill you. Grief is *not* your friend.

"Grief is an evil spirit and it's a selfish emotion." Yes. To both. As a believer, I know there's a Heaven and a hell. I know there are angels and demons. I know there are evil spirits. And grief is one.

And yes, grief is also a selfish emotion. Very selfish. I know. I can hear the uproar over that statement from here. But it is.

Think about it. When you're fighting grief, what are you focused on? The person or thing you've lost? No, because that's already been your focus.

After the loss, you're focused on yourself. On how the grief is making you feel. On what the grief is doing to you. On your pain. At least that was my experience.

And focusing on yourself to the exclusion of everything and everybody else? That's the height of selfishness. Selfishness is about "self." Grief forces you to focus on nothing *but* yourself, thereby making you selfish.

Selfishness was the reason I wasn't reaching out; why I wasn't communicating with anyone; why I was isolating myself. Why I always answered when anyone asked me how I was doing, "*Oh I'm good.*" I wasn't. I was so far from good . . .

I was selfish.

"To defeat our enemy we must first understand him . . . we must develop counter-strategies and tactics of our own . . . our strategies and tactics must be at a much higher level than his . . . minimizing him. This approach . . . gives us both time and space (breathing room)."

Grief is our enemy. This reads like a military strategy. That's because it is. In order to defeat grief, you have to fight grief. And as in any war, if you allow your enemy to get too close, he will kill you. That's how victory is decided in war. The victor is the one who kills more of his enemy.

So also, as in war, to defeat grief, you must understand it. You must develop strategies and tactics that are on a higher level than the grief's strategies and tactics, and you must do all of this to buy yourself the time and rest you need to kill it. You must become a grief killer.

Begin with the end in mind. That's a Steven Covey principle from his book *The 7 Habits of Highly Effective People*. And it's appropriate here.

The end, in this case, is for you to kill the grief. And by killing it, to be able to rise above it and move past it, to transform your life.

So the **REAL** end is that. Transforming your life after loss.

The title of the book is *Transforming Your Life AFTER Loss*. Not during loss. Not before loss. But after the loss occurs. And part of that is killing the grief that manifests after the loss.

Like loss, grief also has by-products. These are secondary effects that occur because of the grief. One is guilt.

➤ GUILT WILL KILL YOU, TOO

I referenced this earlier. I would lay awake at night replaying all the stuff that had happened in my head. Every decision I'd made. Every interaction I'd had, both with family members, hospital staff and hospice employees.

Asking myself over and over again, "Did I do enough? Could I have done more? What if we'd caught it earlier? How would we have caught it earlier? Did I give her enough attention? Did I do the right things with her? Did I neglect her? Should I have had all those people around her? The hospice people made me tell her she was in hospice; should I have just told them no? It scared her when I told her that. Why did I?"

And on and on and on. For me, it was an endless loop. And if you let it, the guilt will eat you up and kill you too. The good news, though, is that once you kill the grief, the guilt goes too.

Finally, as yet another by-product of the grief, there's what I call the Gray Zone. I've already talked about it some.

➤ THE GRAY ZONE

It's what happens when the world just looks and feels gray. Drab. No color. No life. No joy. No happiness. No fun. No anything. It's apathy and yet it's more than apathy. You have no desire to do anything, go anywhere, or see or talk to anyone. Food loses its flavor and its appeal.

Sleep isn't refreshing; you're as exhausted when you wake up after 10 or 12 hours of sleep as you were before you went to bed. Nothing feels good. You don't take care of yourself. Personal hygiene can become a distant memory. Alcohol isn't an escape; it just makes it all worse; it magnifies it.

The Gray Zone is where stupid decisions—that seem rational at the time—get made. It's also where bad things happen. Death happens in the Gray Zone. Remember when I said that grief wants to kill you? This is where it happens. How doesn't matter; it's just a detail. It's the where in this case that's important: the Gray Zone.

But kill the grief, and the Gray Zone dissipates. Color is restored, excitement and passion become real again. Life returns.

Ughhh! That was intense. And **NOT** pleasant. But *grief* isn't pleasant. It's not an escape. And anyone that tries to tell you otherwise is lying. Fight it for all you're worth. Become a grief killer.

Your life depends on it.

That's it for this one. The next chapter will be short. I'm going to just touch on how grief can change you.

It's a bit of a breather. I need one and I'm sure you do too. This one is *Secret #6*, called *"Grief Changes You—Sometimes Permanently"* and is the lead into the final chapter on grief.

See you in there.

SECRET

Six

Grief Changes You— Sometimes Permanently

"The good news, though, is that once you kill the grief, the guilt goes too." This line is from the last chapter, somewhere in the final third of it, where I'm talking about one of the major by-products of grief, which is guilt.

When I say that grief changes you, what I mean is that it changes you internally. It always starts with your emotions. Your emotions then affect how your physical body feels. The feeling in your physical body affects and impacts your thinking; what your thoughts are.

Then it becomes an endless loop. Negative emotions lead to feeling bad in your body which leads to bad thinking; this is the cycle.

There are lots of negative emotions, but only four core emotions and all of these negative emotions come from three of the four. They stem from sadness, fear and anger. Happiness is the fourth core emotion, but that doesn't play yet.

Consider depression and guilt. Those probably stem from the base emotion of sadness, although guilt may also be rooted in fear. Fight, flight, freeze or faint are the classic responses to fear, but fight may also be related to anger. Lashing out certainly is. Hatred probably also comes from anger.

What about despair? Sadness, more than likely.

And so on. I'm sure you can think of others you've dealt with or are dealing with.

But grief can change you. And sometimes it can change you permanently. Hatred and anger are probably the most destructive, and once rooted, are probably also the hardest to get rid of. These emotions almost become defense mechanisms; you start to believe they're protecting you from losing your mind.

But they can become a form of mind-loss in and of themselves.

What's the old saying? "If it's true, it's not paranoia. They really ARE out to get me."

Something like this can occur within your emotions. Then, as a result of all of this, these negative emotions affect how your body feels. And they don't make your body feel good, do they?

My experience has been that the mind follows the body. If the body feels good, thoughts are generally good. If the body feels bad, same parallel with thoughts. Then once your body feels bad, your thoughts go bad; they get dark. People are always waiting for the other shoe to drop.

Then these feelings and behavior normalize. They become

the place from where a person functions. You may know people, who no matter how good they have it, are always able to find the negative.

I didn't really understand how someone could do this until I started doing it myself.

The catalyst for me was grief.

But the **REAL** catalyst was the loss which created that grief.

The point is this. Transform your life after the loss, and grief won't have a chance to gain the foothold it requires to change you. Which is the whole point of this book.

Because left unchecked, it will. And it will change you forever; probably in ways you don't want to be changed.

I came close to being changed in ways I didn't want to be changed. I came close to becoming a hateful, negative and mean person. I experienced some of it. My behavior reflected it.

And I didn't like myself when I was like that. Which led to more guilt, which led to more feeling bad physically, which led to more dark thoughts, which led to bad actions and interactions with others.

I know I hurt people during this time. And then, you guessed it, I felt even more guilt over that, which led to more . . . you get the picture.

This is another reason why it's so critical not to merely cope with grief, but to absolutely kill it. To disappear it. To totally get it out of your life.

If a person tries to manage grief, it'll end up managing them. In fact, it'll end up running—and ruining—their entire life.

So don't allow that. Put your foot down. Decide and act.

Kill it. Become a Grief Killer.

Okay. Got *that* off my chest. And I caught my breath. Told you it was short.

I'm ready for *Secret #7: "Grief isn't A Process—Part Two."*

How about you?

Ready?

If so, I'll see you in there.

Seven

Grief Isn't A Process

Part Two

In this chapter that I want to talk about being a Grief Killer and finding your way through the Grief Curve™.

But before I get into that, I want to say a few words about emotions.

In the previous chapter, I was mentioned the core emotions, and of the four of them—fear, sadness, anger and happiness— three were negative. And those were the ones I focused on.

Don't get me wrong; happiness does have a place in all of this, because that's where joy lives, and we'll get to it. Just not right here or right now.

I classified 75% of the core emotions as "negative" because that's how most people see emotions. As either bad or good. Negative or positive.

But I want you to shift, perhaps even evolve, your thinking a bit with this next thought. And that is this.

When it comes to emotions, there are neither positive nor negative emotions. No such thing as bad or good. There are just emotions.

People *qualify* them as negative or positive, because of the way they make us feel, and because that makes it easier for them to be put into a box and understood. Humans are always wanting to quantify and qualify everything.

So, sadness might make us cry. And for men especially, crying is a societal and cultural no-no. It's considered a sign of weakness and men aren't supposed to show weakness. Of course, the act of crying might just be a form of pressure release, and it might actually lead to feeling what's quantified as good. *(It does, you know.)*

Give this concept some thought in your quiet time. Then, start looking at emotions with a sense of curiosity; with a *"hmmm, I wonder . . ."* attitude instead of with instant judgment; of being either good or bad, positive or negative.

I've learned some things. One, by looking at it this way, it will calm you when it comes to emotions. Two, it makes it much easier to understand and accept the waves that emotions are, and that they come in. Three, it makes it easier to let them all the way in, and to feel them all the way through.

It makes it easier when you feel an emotion start to build, to let it build, then crest and recede, because you know what to expect from it; you already know what it's going to do. That takes the fear of the unknown out of it, and allows you to experience it, to feel it fully and get through it.

Allowing your emotions to build, crest and recede is to accept them. And by accepting, you're not fighting; you're not struggling. Not fighting means it doesn't take nearly as much energy to deal with it, so you aren't exhausted.

In fact, that curious attitude, that *"hmmm, I wonder . . ."* approach, will make not just emotions, but also life in general, much easier to accept and understand. This is primarily because it takes the focus off you and puts the focus onto the thing or the person that you're curious about. By being genuinely curious, you destroy that judgmental side we're so quick to apply to situations, circumstances, or people.

Try it.

PRO TIP: When practicing genuine curiosity, actually make the *"hmmm"* sound out loud . . . maybe even the *"hmmm"* sound combined with *"I wonder what's going on here . . ."*

Love to hear your feedback on it.

➢ Grief Killer

Alright. Onto Grief Killer.

"This is another reason it's so critical not to merely cope with grief, but to absolutely kill it. To disappear it. To totally get it out of your life.

If a person tries to manage grief, it'll end up managing them. In fact, it'll end up running—and ruining—their entire life.

So don't allow that. Put your foot down. Decide and act.

Kill it. Become a Grief Killer."

This is a passage from the last chapter, *Secret #6: Grief Changes You,* which builds on *Secret #5: Grief Isn't a Process.* And which we'll expand on here for just a bit.

Honestly, I've already said pretty much everything I have to say about becoming a Grief Killer. The importance of it. The reasoning behind it. Everything maybe, except *how* to do it.

Well, the how is this: by transforming your life. By not accepting that grief is permanent, or that it has to be a way of life. By not getting "stuck." Either in grief or in the past. I'm going to talk more about being stuck in the past in *Secret #10: The Way Out*. But for now, just "decide and act" to not get stuck. Do whatever it takes to keep moving forward. Don't stop. Never quit.

I don't know about you, but when I'm driving and using my GPS, and I see that I'm about to get caught in a traffic jam, I'll try and find an alternate route. I'd rather keep moving, even it if eventually takes a little longer, than sit there, stuck in traffic.

Not everyone feels that way. I do. I want to keep moving. Always.

Same for weather hampering travel when I'm flying. I'd rather do something than just sit and be stuck.

And I think that's the remedy for being stuck in either grief or the past.

Do something.

And most often, when it's possible, do something that involves helping, assisting or being of service to other people.

Why? When you're bogged down in grief, the last thing you feel like doing is helping someone else. But that's the time you might want to consider it. Because by focusing on someone else, it takes you out of yourself; it kills the selfishness by taking the attention off yourself and putting it onto someone else.

That's one of the things I did. I volunteered. A lot. Because I found that when I did that, I felt better. I felt useful. And it was appreciated by the organizations I volunteered for.

Another of my "do somethings" was the Never Quit decision. Once I decided that I wasn't going to quit, I had to create actions that matched up with that. Whether that was just getting up, cleaning up and getting dressed, there were actions I took that were just that: actions. Decide and act.

This is so critical.

Another step in killing grief, is understanding what it is and how it affects you.

➤ THE GRIEF CURVE

I'm both a visual and a kinetic learner. That means I learn by seeing, and then I really figure it out by doing. So to satisfy my visual side, when it came to understanding grief, I created the Grief Curve™.

The diagram is on the next page.

Look it over, then I'll explain it.

It's a visual representation of what happens when a person experiences or is thrown into grief.

Do something.

This is the Grief Curve™. It's a visual representation of what happened to me when I was hit with grief after the sudden death of my wife.

Let's take it piece by piece, shall we? And don't be overwhelmed by it. There's lots of little pieces to it, because there's lots of pieces and elements to grief.

Let's go.

The upper left is the POD or point of death. *(I like acronyms. That probably stems from my Marine Corps background . . . boy,*

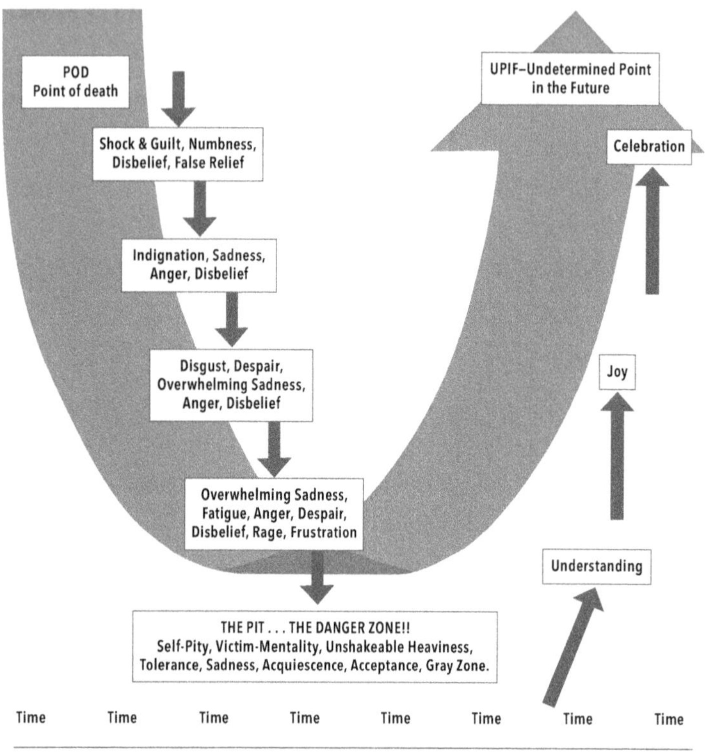

Download a Full Size PDF of the Grief Curve at https://craftmethodcoaching.com/griefcurve.

do we love acronyms!) Then you see the downward-pointing arrows, and the dialogue boxes either below or next to them.

Inside the dialogue boxes, you see words, and the words are all emotions.

Let's take at the first dialogue box, right below the POD box. In that box you see the words shock & guilt, numbness, disbelief and false relief. These are all of the things that I felt at the time of my wife's death.

Below that you see another box. Inside of it are the words indignation, sadness, anger, disbelief.

The third box contains disgust, despair, overwhelming sadness (not just sadness), anger & disbelief. Finally, in the fourth box, it's overwhelming sadness, fatigue, anger, despair, disbelief, rage & frustration.

Inside each box, when I listed these emotions, I tried to list them in the order I felt them. This was three months from the time of her death, so I was still very, very close to it and in the throes of extreme grief.

Remember when I said humans try to quantify the chaos that is grief? Most people try to do it with the stages of grief I mentioned earlier. This is my methodology for quantifying it. I HAD to understand it; to wrap my mind around it. This helped me do that.

But at this time in my life, I was at the bottom of the curve, and either in, or fast approaching the fifth box. My sense is that I was already in The Pit: The Danger Zone, and creating the Curve was one of my "do somethings" to try and get myself out.

I knew that if I stayed stuck here—and I felt like there was a high chance of that happening—I might never get out. This is where the Gray Zone lives. This is where death is.

Along the bottom of the Curve you'll see a bar with the words "time" repeated over and over from left to right. That's because this didn't happen all at once, it occurred over time.

Let me say something about time here. When you're caught in the Grief Curve™ time is different. It changes. And by changing, I mean it really has little to no significance. Days and nights; weeks and months . . . they just kind of run together. It feels like time isn't passing; like the clock has literally slowed to a crawl, but it still keeps going. Time gets really weird.

What I want you to notice is the steepness of the downward

angle. It's less of a slide, and much more of a fall into the curve. It's also a seriously steep upward climb.

What I found was that it was a heck of a lot easier to fall down into the curve, than it was to get out.

See my point?

After the pit—which by the way, is flat making it easy to stay down there—is the climb out.

It's steep, as you can see. To put that in perspective, when a 747 passenger jet takes off, the maximum climb out angle is 15 degrees. A fighter jet is roughly sixty degrees. The angle of the climb-out of the Grief Curve™ is 80+ degrees. And straight up is ninety degrees.

So. it's almost a straight up climb, on a smooth surface with no handholds or cracks, to get out.

You have to be a lot stronger to muscle your way up out of the pit than you do to fall/slide down into it.

But after the pit comes understanding, then eventually joy and after that comes celebration. That's at the UPIF. The Undetermined Point In The Future.

Because as neat and clean as this diagram of the Grief Curve™ is, in real life, it's neither. It's not neat, nor is it clean. It's a mess and it's messy. It's nasty, dirty, hard. All of that and more.

But this gives you some idea of what I experienced and am experiencing now, by the way.

Because you have to remember, when I drew this, I was in the Pit; in the Danger Zone. I was at the bottom of the Grief Curve™. I had yet to make my way out of it.

But I did. I haven't looked at this graphic since early 2020. But I can see that I DID experience understanding, joy and celebration. In fact, I'm experiencing the last two now, and I will for the rest of my life.

Because I understand—because I lived them—all the dynamics about which I've written and will write. I know what this this monster is, where it lives, and I know how to kill it.

And now you do, too.

We'll continue with the next chapter, which is the beginning of the "actionable," or the things you can do not only to continue to climb out of the Grief Curve™, but also to reinforce those actions and make sure you never go back.

I'm done talking about grief in this book. Can we agree that you and I are both Grief Killers?

Good.

I'll see you in the next chapter which is *Secret #8: Get Comfortable Being* UN-*Comfortable.*

Eight

Get Comfortable Being *Un*-Comfortable

I want to take a moment here since we just finished the section on grief (and since we're slightly over halfway through the Secrets) and ask you something:

Is this making sense to you? Are you seeing how this stackable concept works?

First, there are the foundational steps of Wanting and Willing; Deciding and Acting; and Understanding It Can Be Lost.

Then, we stack on Surrendering and Never Quitting. Next, you read the three Grief Chapter which are the explanatory pieces.

Finally, you have these last few chapters. Secrets 8 through 13 are the action chapters; they outline and explain the things you can actually do to jump-start transforming your life after loss.

Are you seeing how it all fits together?

And more importantly, are you seeing how knowing these

things gives you tools, power and strength? Maybe even encouragement to keep forging ahead?

If you do, that's awesome, because that was my goal for you! I wanted the foundational and explanatory chapters to provide a base of understanding, ownership, and acceptance that you can take with you into the action chapters.

I hope you're feeling better about everything, after the first half of this book. Let's lock that in with the rest.

Of course, I get it if understanding, ownership, and acceptance aren't quite there for you yet. Maybe you're on the cusp of them, but they're still kind of around the corner for you.

If that's you, I'd like you to do something. (See? Action chapter, lol.)

I'd like you to send me a quick email at john@craftmethod-coaching.com telling me where you're stuck or what you're not quite getting. I promise I'll respond. It's important that you gain understanding, ownership, and acceptance before we get into the rest of it, so if you're struggling in one of those areas, please let me know.

We'll work through it together.

Okay. This shouldn't be a very long chapter. Because it's really pretty simple.

Remember, there are some non-negotiables, when it comes to transforming your life after loss.

We've talked about a couple of them, but this is a big one.

And it's what the title of this secret is. You must get _comfortable_ being _uncomfortable_.

The reason for this is simple. It's because none of this stuff that you're doing, or that you're reading, or that you're dealing with, is easy.

It's all hard. It's uncomfortable. It's not like you're kicking back in your recliner, just skimming through this book with no effort. Every page takes you out of your comfort zone. It puts you into a place of uncomfortableness.

But that's also what loss does. It makes you uncomfortable. You've lost someone. Or something. Whatever you lost was important to you.

Now it's gone. It's no longer yours. No longer there. Your life will never be the same. And change is never easy.

People who say they thrive on change? I'm not sure I believe them. Because I used to be one of them.

Generally speaking, people who say they thrive on change are just bored. And they're bored because whatever it is they're doing isn't their passion. It's not their purpose.

When you're focused on your purpose and your passion, you can never be bored. You've probably heard the saying, *"If you do what you love, you'll never work a day in your life."*

What that's really saying though, is that if you're passionate about something—or if you're pursuing your purpose—it's a joy to do it. It doesn't matter how hard it is or how time-consuming or how much effort it requires.

Passion and purpose negate all of that.

One of my passions is writing. When I'm writing, time flies. I'll sit down in the morning and start writing and before I know it, it's suppertime. Or dinner. Or whatever you call it in your house.

And even though I may be uncomfortable when I first start writing, I do it anyway. I never know where the story will go. I mean, I have an outline, so I have an idea of a beginning, a middle and an ending, but I don't know what's going to happen until I sit down and write the words.

But I get comfortable doing it. I've been a writer long enough that I know when it's the right book at the right time, the words will be there. If I start writing something, and the words don't come? It's not writer's block; it's not the right book or maybe not the right time. So maybe it really is "righter's block."

Part of getting comfortable being uncomfortable is experience. It's doing it over and over. Day in and day out.

Part of it is understanding that you're uncomfortable now, and you're intentionally putting yourself in that place so you can become comfortable later. It's a learning curve. A learning curve is always up. It's work.

But it's also growth. And as the saying goes, there's no room to grow inside your comfort zone. When wine makers plant their vineyards, you'll hear them say they want to stress the vines just enough. Depending on the soil, the weather and the other growing conditions, they want those vines to have to work to produce the grapes. The vines that get stressed just enough—that are uncomfortable—produce the best grapes. Naturally, these make the best wine.

That applies to us, too. When we're in an uncomfortable place, that's us getting just the right amount of pressure to produce the best fruit. To produce our best wine.

And when we learn to get comfortable there, when we know that it's okay for us to be in an uncomfortable situation because we know how to get through it, that brings a quiet confidence that others can see and sense. They know something's different about us, but they usually don't know what it is.

But because we've learned how to become comfortable being uncomfortable, that brings them comfort.

Crazy, huh?

So work on it. Intentionally put yourself in uncomfortable (for you) situations, then figure out how you can get comfortable in those.

They say that artificial intelligence, AI, is self-teaching and self-learning. But you don't need AI because you have *organic* intelligence. You also have instincts and your gut, along with reasoning and analytic capabilities. Use all of these. Push your own envelope. You'll figure it out.

If I can do it, seriously . . . those who are determined to certainly can, as well.

A situation that has always been uncomfortable for me is attending the dreaded dinner party or business mixer. I'm not a small-talk kind of guy. It's hard for me. So when I go to these social events—and I do—I go into them knowing that it'll be uncomfortable for me. I also know that if I'm the guy who goes up to others and introduces myself, I can get comfortable very quickly, and I can change what was a negative dynamic into a very positive, even powerful, dynamic.

While underneath there's a current of uncomfortableness, I know how to get comfortable in those situations.

And when I'm comfortable being uncomfortable, I'm also unstoppable. People remember me. They wonder who I am and what I have.

And they'll do that with you, too.

Because frankly, when most people are uncomfortable, it shows. And the world can see it. They're like a negative vortex and nobody wants to be around them. Next time you're in a social or business situation, look around. Find that lone wolf in the corner. Most likely they'll have a frown on their face, or they'll be checking their phone and not engaging with anyone . . . phones are great for that. They'll also be by themselves. That's because they're uncomfortable and they don't know how to flip the script.

Now you do.

So do it.

Now let's look at loss. When you understand, own, and accept whatever loss you've experienced, when you're in that uncomfortable place, when you consciously look for ways to do it, you'll figure out how to make yourself comfortable in your uncomfortableness. And because you do, you'll grow.

This entire *Transforming Your Life After Loss* thing . . . the book, the podcast, the keynote speech, the workshops, the coaching, all of it; it's all been born out of uncomfortableness. It was born because I refused to stay in that loss paradigm; I refused to settle.

I was—and I am—determined to turn all of this into something good. I have a victory mindset. And it's not just a mindset, either. It's a knowing; an attitude.

But this all came out of devastating loss, debilitating grief, and then the recovery and restoration that occurred after. I'll talk more about recovery and restoration in *Secret #11: The Road Less Traveled.*

For now, let's leave it at that.

It's time to move onto *Secret #9: The Power of Discovery.*

See you in there.

The Power of Discovery

So, work on it. Intentionally put yourself in uncomfortable (for you) situations, then figure out/learn how you can get comfortable in those.

They say that artificial intelligence, AI, is self-teaching and self-learning. But you don't need AI, because you have **organic** intelligence. You also have instinct and your gut, along with reasoning and analytic capabilities. Use all of these. Push your own envelope. You'll figure it out.

. . . I was—and I am—determined to turn all this into something good. I have a victory mindset. And it's not just a mindset, either. It's a **knowing; an attitude**.

But this came out of devastating loss, debilitating grief, and then the recovery and restoration that occurred after.

You may recognize the above passage from the last chapter.

What I don't say implicitly—but certainly allude to—I'll say very clearly here.

NONE of this happens without the process of discovery.

None of it.

Discovery has been the underlying key to transforming *my* life, and it'll be the underlying key to transforming *your* life as well.

Count on it.

We're kind of like Christopher Columbus. He set out without maps and without charts across a vast, unknown ocean. All he had to guide him were two things. The first was a general sense of direction; he knew he needed to head west.

Ish.

The second thing he had though, was his gut. He simply knew-that-he-knew-that-he-knew there was a New World out there, and that he was the man who was destined to discover it.

That's us, isn't it? We have a sense of the direction we need to head. Ish. Then we have our gut telling us and we just KNOW that it's there, waiting. Waiting for us to discover it.

If we didn't have those two things, I doubt we'd do anything with it.

I know that's true in my case. I knew kind of which direction to head, and I also knew I needed to discover what the path to transforming my life was.

➤ THE QUESTIONS

Let me take a quick left turn here. I get asked a lot about the process of discovery. Some of it I can explain. Some of it I can't.

That's because it's personal and maybe a bit mysterious. And everybody's discovery process is unique to them.

That said, there is a tried-and-true method for getting started on the path to discovery. It will work 100% of the time. It's not hard either.

That method is to ask questions. What questions, you're wondering? Any question. All questions. Nothing is off limits. As you identify questions, your mind, and particularly your subconscious, will start attuning itself to finding answers. I'd recommend keeping a notepad, your phone or some other method of jotting stuff down handy and with you, because what you'll find is that you'll start discovering answers to those questions. They'll start coming. And oftentimes, they don't come at opportune moments. They'll come in the middle of a conversation. They'll wake you up. You might even dream some of the answers. I have.

But the key? Ask questions. Of yourself. Of others. Of Google. It doesn't matter. Just start asking. It always works.

Try it. Test it. Then let me know what you . . . discover.

When I was in the thick of it after my loss, I started analyzing grief and writing a book called Grief Killer. I never published it, and I doubt I ever will. But it started with questions.

Why? Because it wasn't so much a book as it was a rant. It was me screaming my guts out onto the pages; it's primal, man. It's pretty much nothing but raw emotion about how I was feeling. And I think it was my therapy. It's one of the things that got me out of the Pit, out of the Danger Zone of the Grief Curve™; out of the Gray Zone.

So, I don't think it's for publication. But it WAS a process of discovery. That was when I discovered and developed the Grief Curve™ as well. Another discovery.

I decided a year or two later that I was going to look into becoming a certified life-coach. I've always been a coach in business, with my sellers in the radio business, but I knew there was a lot I didn't know. So, I set out to discover that. I became certified through Brave Thinking Institute. I like their curriculum, and their curriculum sparked and inspired me to create my own material. Another discovery.

Constant questions. Constant discoveries.

After working with my two coaches and talking about this with them, they fed me their thoughts and impressions, leading me to do . . . what?

You guessed it! Discover!

And out of **THOSE** conversations, the resulting questions and the discovery process, TYLAL *(Transform Your Life After Loss)* was born.

It ALL began with my loss, and everything that came after that.

Meaning, all of the discovery.

Here's something else I discovered:

Anything that's *anything,* was born out of uncomfortableness, and because whoever was in that state refused to stay stuck there, they refused to settle. They pushed forward and discovered their way out. Think Christopher Columbus.

Think *you.* Because that's what you're in the process of doing. You're pushing forward. You're questioning. You're discovering. All are crucial.

But here's the thing you can expect, so be ready for it: The whole path is NEVER revealed all at once. You'll discover one thing and develop or work on it. Somewhere in there, that'll lead to another discovery. Then you'll repeat the process. Over and over, until finally, your path is clear and you know you're on it.

Then you'll discover something else, and your path will change slightly—or greatly. Doesn't matter. The point is the point. Discovery will lead you to your path, wherever it leads.

What matters is the discovery. Discovery will lead you to your destiny and your destination. It's why it's so important.

➤ THE TWO STATES

When I look back on all of this; at the steps I've taken to get here; on the things that have happened; and the things that have NOT happened; all of it . . . I see the path looking back. It's as clear as day.

But I also see the two states of being. Really, there are only two. The first one is peace. The second, chaos. All things stem from both. When you're happy, content, satisfied, joyful, you're coming to those things from a place of peace. Internally and externally.

But when you're stressed, angry, sad, depressed or hurt . . . those come from a place of chaos. Internally and externally.

For me, the discovery process is so integral to living from and in a place of peace, not chaos. Another way to define this concept is to use the terms expansive and constricted.

I mentioned what I saw when I looked back. Looking forward though? I mean, I have a sense of where this will take me, but I know that I'll remain flexible and fluid, because I also know that I'll continue discovering things that will either strengthen or alter it. And by alter, what I really mean, is to take it to a much higher level, much faster.

I'm experiencing exponential growth with this. The people who are close to me watching this can't believe how fast it's happening now.

But what they didn't see was the incubation period. That took a while for me.

Look. You may have an incubation period, or you may not. You may take a couple of years to get going, or you may not. Remember, I didn't have a resource like me when I was moving onto my path. When I was discovering all of this.

My sincere hope is that I can help speed up the process a bit for you by revealing the secrets that I've what?

That I've DISCOVERED!

My other sincere hope is that by reading this, internalizing, and making it your own, is that you will gain the confidence to move ahead, to do the discovery necessary to transform your life. I want you to understand, own and accept it.

You see, part of what held me back and got in my way (another discovery) was me. I had a crisis of confidence. I was so shaken up by what had happened, that as I mentioned earlier, I forgot (but what I really mean is that I lost) who I was.

And when that happened, all of the attributes that make me, *me*—they were lost as well.

My confidence, my surety, my problem-solving skills, my drive, my ambition, my . . . well, you get the idea . . . all of that was gone, too.

Loss isn't about just one loss; it's about losses squared or multiplied significantly.

And here's another discovery: One loss always leads to other losses. Always. It's the nature of loss.

So, if by writing this book and doing all the attendant stuff with it I can help you eliminate your own crisis of confidence, I want to.

Because you'll discover more and grow much more quickly being confident than you will being like I was. By being namby-pamby. By feeling sorry for yourself. By having a victim mentality rather than having an attitude of victory.

Back to our friend Christopher Columbus for a second. Do you think that when he set out on an unknown ocean that he ever had the mindset of being lost at sea, of sinking, of being destroyed or killed? Did he have an attitude of defeat?

No! Of course not!

He had the mindset and the attitude of victory. Remember, he *KNEW* he was going to discover the New World; he just had to get there.

CC had the mind of a victor, of a champion, not the mindset of a victim. He was a champ, not a chump. And he knew it. If he'd thought of himself as a victim, he never would have set out on the journey.

No matter what has happened in your life, you are NOT a victim. Get that one down deep. Understand, own, and accept it. You're not a victim; you're a Victor. And yes, that's with a capital "V!"

I want this book to give YOU the champion mindset; the attitude of a Victor. Someone who knows they've already won and just has to complete the discovery process to actualize and manifest it.

You ARE a Victor. How do I know? Because you wouldn't have come this far if you weren't.

And discovery is an essential tool in your toolbox. One you can't do without. It's what will move you onto and down your path one step at a time.

I talk about revealing secrets in the title of this book. How do you think I know them? I discovered them.

Well, discovery is what reveals YOUR secretes; those things that you need to learn and do along with the places you need to go in order to transform your life.

Okay.

These are action chapters. Meaning I want you to take some action before we move onto the next one.

For this chapter, I'd like you to get a piece of paper out—no, scratch that. Time to get serious. Time to commit and get dedicated.

➤ The Steps

IF you're serious about transforming your life, then do this:

1. Get a spiral bound notebook or a fairly big journal.
   (I personally like a 9.5x7 size.)
2. At the beginning, write "Beginning." (Rocket science, huh? LOL!)
3. Then, jot down a few sentences describing what your life is like now, and specifically, what you'd like to change.
4. Then go to the next page. Write down the word "End."
   (You're doing this not because it's the end, but because you're Beginning (where you are today) with the End (what you want your transformed life to be) in mind.

5. Under "End," describe what your transformed life looks like. **IMPORTANT:** *Write this as though it's already happened!* Specifically, write what you've changed from the Beginning and what you really love about your new life. Not "like." LOVE. That's an important distinction. Don't worry about the "how." That'll come. Right now, just define the "what."

6. Finally, on the next page, write the word "Discoveries."

7. Think about what's happened since you started reading this book. Write down any discoveries you've made or any that come to you now; either about yourself, your situation or circumstances, or your future. (Don't write a book; just key words or concepts; you'll go back to those later.)

8. On the next page write down as a header "Next Steps." Write down a few things you think you can do, or things you want to do to start the process.

9. Now you've got a template. You know where you are. You know where you want to go. Ish. You've made some discoveries, and you've got a couple of next steps to pursue; some "do somethings." This is the beginning of your transformed life.

You're discovering for yourself what your process will be.

Stay alive and sensitive to your discovery process. Every time you make one, come back here and write it down, along with the associated next steps that discovery will inevitably lead to.

You can do this. And this is a hack; it's a shortcut.

Man! If only I'd had this process all along . . .

Don't shine this action on. Do it. It may take you 15 minutes, maybe an hour. You may have to go to the store and get a journal.

That's okay. Do it. It'll be time and money well spent.

Once you've done that, I'll be waiting for you in the next chapter. It's *Secret#10: The Way Out.* You're gonna like it. A lot.

I can't wait to hear about what you're discovering! I'll see you in there.

Ten

THE WAY OUT

Ah. We're getting closer to the end of the book, which will actually be the beginning of your new life. Of your *transformed* life!

In this chapter, *"The Way Out,"* I'm going to give you exactly that. I'll detail the two steps you'll take to get out of wherever it is you are right now, so you can catapult yourself into wherever it is you want to be.

Please note that I said "catapult." Not "ease into it." Not tentatively "dip your toe in the water." But CATAPULT into it. The general definition of the word "catapult" is this: *mechanism for forcefully propelling stones, spears, or other projectiles.*

And while we won't be hurling any stones, spears or other projectiles here, YOU will be forcefully propelling YOURSELF into your transformed life by doing the two things I'll describe and explain here.

But first . . .

Remember.

All of this is stackable. You're stacking one concept and action step on top of another, and you're building this edifice that's your new life, on top of an extremely strong and unshakeable foundation.

So . . . let's review a bit from the last chapter, shall we?

Write down "Beginning." Jot down a few sentences describing what your life is like now and specifically, what you'd like to change. Write down the word "End." Describe what your transformed life looks like . . . don't worry about the "how." That'll come. Right now, just define the "what."

Did you do this? Did you get your journal? And do the Discoveries page along with the Next Steps page?

Because if you didn't, I'm going to ask that before you continue, please go back and do so.

Or not.

That's your decision. So, decide. Then act. One way or the other.

Yes, this is an accountability question. It's the first time I've asked one in this entire process. And I'm asking it now for a simple reason.

If you can't—or won't—do this, then you won't transform your life, and there's simply no reason for you to continue with the rest of the secrets.

So, I'm holding you accountable here. Because I believe that transforming your life IS something you want to do. And sometimes it's easy to get caught up in, *"I'll go back and do it later."* Do you know how many times I've said that? (Many.)

Do you know how many times I've actually gone back and done it later?

Maybe 2% of the time. And that's a big maybe. But mainly, I didn't.

So, this is your second chance.

If you're gonna do this, do it right. And doing it right, is doing it now. So, if you got caught up in the "Do it later" trap, I'm giving you the opportunity to fix it.

To do it right, by doing it now.

This is a very specific and on-going activity. It's easy to do and it's easy to measure. That's intentional.

But you *must* do it for it to work.

So. Did you?

I'll wait for you. No problem.

But do it.

Okay. Great! Let's move on.

I referenced that there are two things I'll cover in this chapter. Here they are.

➤ Leave the Past Behind

Number one is to leave the past behind. The second one is to get out of your head.

Doing these two things are transformational in a way that very few others are. Let me explain how.

Understanding, owning, and accepting these two dynamics, then actually DOING them, is a *huge* leap forward into transforming your life; into creating the life you want and the life you'd love to have.

Let's start with number one: leaving the past behind. I wrote an article a couple of years ago called *"Lose My Number—The Past"* all about leaving the past behind.

But it's too long for this book, so I'll pull a few thoughts from it.

When you get hit with a loss, it's like being ambushed by the enemy. Even if you see it coming (like I did) the fight is on. And this is a fight you lose. This is your loss.

When the loss happens, a lot of other things start to happen, as well. Grief sets in. Other losses occur. You can list it out; we've already been over it.

But there's one thing you're probably doing. It's what I did.

I started living in the past. This is natural. It's normal. Why? Because the past is "pre-loss." It's before you got ambushed; before you got hit. And living in the past is a protective move and defense mechanism. It's something people do to try to mitigate or reduce the pain, hurt, and fear they're feeling and dealing with. Because "in the past" is where all the good stuff happened. Here in the present is where all the bad stuff is happening. So of course, we're going to slide right back into where there was no pain, where it was perfect. Where it was all butterflies and rainbows.

Except that it wasn't.

When this happens, humans have a filter that slides down over their mind's-eye, and it blocks out all the stuff that wasn't good. So, we don't have to focus on the bad. In comparison to our present, to the loss we've endured, the past was perfect. Or so we tell ourselves.

Which means we're lying to ourselves. And in order to transform your life, if I haven't said it yet (and I don't think I have) I'll say it now.

You must face the truth.

The truth of your loss. The truth of your hurt; of your pain.

The truth of your changed circumstances or situation. And the truth of your past, too.

The truth is this: your past *wasn't* all butterflies and rainbows. There was imperfection; there was pain. There just wasn't as much of it then as you're dealing with and experiencing now.

It's also not as fresh, or maybe not as extreme. The human brain isn't wired to remember pain as much as it is to remember pleasure. If we remembered pain to the point that we felt it, there would be no childbirth.

Think about it for a moment.

And I'm not saying that you can't have memories, or that you can't visit them from time to time. Of course you can. And you will. You won't be able to stop them.

The key, though, is in visiting them from "time to time" like you would a favorite relative. Not moving in and living there. When people start to take up residence there, in the past, is when they get stuck.

If you remember the Grief Curve™ you'll remember what I designated as "The Pit—The Danger Zone" at the bottom of the curve. It's the place where people get stuck. I've got seven attributes listed there, but I should add an eighth one: being stuck in the past.

That's dangerous. Because being stuck in the past destroys all hope for the future. It also robs people of all of their power. This is where depression, extreme sadness, the Gray Zone, all of that, come from.

The problem with going back to the past and staying there is that the past becomes the focal point of living. And no one has the ability to really go back to the past or to change anything that happened.

That's where hope gets destroyed and where power gets robbed. Because when a person is stuck in the past they're powerless to change anything. It's like being caught in the mirror of the evil witch in a fairy tale. You can see what's happening outside of the mirror (the present and future), but you're powerless to do anything. The place in the mirror where you're caught (the past), is too comfortable; it has just enough pleasure attached to it that it steals your motivation to get out of it. Instead, some people just sit down and stay there.

Until they die.

No hope. No power. No motivation. No desire. No excitement. No passion. No fun. No reason to do anything. No nothing. No life.

That's what being stuck in the past does. That's what it is.

If you're going to transform your life, you had better get out of that place; you'd better not get stuck. Because if you have no hope, no power, no motivation or no desire then you simply have no future.

Or at least that's what you tell yourself.

But here's a newsflash. The future will come whether you think it will or not. It's inexorable. Meaning it can't be stopped. You're going to meet your future right . . . now.

Whether you have a part in creating your future though, whether you're a participant or a bystander, is up to you. YOU get to decide whether you stay stuck in the past or not.

When you're living in the present, and you're excited about your future, you DO have hope, power, desire, motivation, excitement, fun . . . you have *everything*, a life, as opposed to nothing.

You have an energy, a vitality, that you just don't have otherwise.

Why do you think I hammered on what my editor calls my journaling exercise so hard? When I asked you to determine your Beginning, your End, and your Next Steps?

It's because you're not only an active participant in your future, but you're also becoming the architect, the designer of it! And what IS the future?

Why, it's your transformed life, of course!

Get it?

But—and this is a BIG but—you *CANNOT* do this, any of it, if you're stuck in the past.

There's a concept called "unhooking." And really, that's just a fancy way of saying, "letting go of your past." One of my coaches teaches it as well. I write about it in depth, in the article called *"Lose My Number—The Past."* I go over exactly how you can do it.

Here's the short version:

So, back to your past. Lose its number. Forget it. When it knocks or calls, don't answer. Don't reply to its texts. Unfriend it.

This whole thing is about moving from what is (your now) into what's ahead (your future). It's about recognizing what you have now, and about focusing on what's ahead.

And if you don't let go of your past, if you don't get "unstuck," you'll never, ever live a rewarding and fulfilling rest of your life. And no matter what's happened, if you're reading this, you DO have a rest of your life to live!

I'm serious. Before you go any further, just make a conscious choice, and say these words out loud as you read them: "I'm letting go—completely—of my past. I will live in my present and I will focus on my future."

Then every time you're tempted to "go back" to that past, remember this moment. Remember where you were when you did this, when you said these words. Say them again.

➤ Get Out of Your Head

Okay. Onto number two: getting out of your head.

I recently had an email conversation with a coaching client that describes this perfectly. This client was absolutely stuck in their head, and they defended themselves and their positions for over an hour.

Because when we're lost in our heads, that's what we do. We think it's the right answer, even when it isn't; even when on some gut level, we KNOW it isn't. So, what do we do? If anybody questions it, we do two things: we get defensive and we dig our heels in. In other words, we get stubborn.

The combination of stubborn and defensive is a tough one. It's a tough place for somebody to be because now they're anything BUT open and curious. They're the opposite. Closed off and stubborn; clinging to their opinions, even when they know they're wrong. It's also difficult for a coach to work with them because they're not being open or curious.

To change, to transform, people must be open and curious. We've discussed this.

So, here's what my coaching to this person was:

The whole purpose of this conversation today had nothing

to do with what you do or don't do. I was pushing you a little for a reason.

The reason and the purpose of the conversation had everything to do with getting you out of your own head—even if it was just for an hour—because nothing good ever happens there. I know. I was stuck there too.

But by focusing on something else besides our situations—anything else—it allows us to start to see what's possible; and once we see that, we want to start taking steps toward changing our situation. We can't help it. Even if it's just baby steps. Enough baby steps, and a person can walk around the world.

But staying stuck in our heads? That all but guarantees we'll never move ahead; we'll do things we know we shouldn't, all the while justifying them to ourselves with convoluted logic, or no logic. Worst is that a year from now, we'll be in the same place—or even further back—as we were a year ago. It's a vicious cycle.

But the cycle can be broken. You've got the ability, the talent, the skills and the power to do that. The first step is remembering who you really are. As my coach told me, **"Feel more. Think less."** Partially meaning: "Get out of your head." This is coaching from such a powerful perspective that I didn't even know I needed it. It's working in my life. And it's changing my world because it's so powerfully life-changing on a fundamental level.

I want you to start seeing what's possible again. And when the word "impossible" crosses your mind, I want you to instantly see it as **"I'm possible"** instead.

It's out there for you, if you want it, and are willing to do the work. Commitment shows out when the person in the conversation just decides to quietly do the work, and then does it.

I think you've got some limiting beliefs that are keeping you from your best life. When you limit yourself to a pre-determined definition based on "how it's always been," it creates problems.

I also want you to start doing something instead of getting stuck in your head all the time, focusing on why stuff won't work, and why your life is so bad, and not doing anything.

The way I see it, you're finally stabilized in your life . . . so now you've got a platform to work from in order to be able to accomplish the next thing. Then the next. And the next. Whatever those "nexts" are.

I want you to be able to find and experience the joy in life again. It's out there, and it can be found no matter where we are. And it should be. Once that joy is regained, it makes things so much easier.

Any of that sound familiar? It should. It's what I believe and teach. More than that, it's what I've lived.

PRO TIP: If you want to get out of your head, focus on helping or doing something for someone else. Volunteering is a good starting place for this. Because when you're stuck in your head, you're focused on you and nothing else. Your situation. Your circumstances. On you.

You're back to the selfish part of grief. So, to counteract this, focus on someone else. Try it. I guarantee you'll notice the difference.

Okay. that's it for this one. You now have two more keys to the kingdom. You have the way out in your hot, little hands.

Use it.

Next up? *Secret #11: The Road Less Traveled.*

See you in there.

SECRET

Eleven

THE ROAD LESS TRAVELED

Hey! Glad you made it!!

This is one of my favorite places. Mainly because I like to go fast; and when I'm on a road that fewer people are on—the road less travelled—for example—I can go as fast as I want.

In all seriousness, though, this is the road you're on. By reading this book and doing the exercises inside, you've put yourself on the road less traveled.

This book isn't for everyone. Just like this road isn't for everyone.

But for those whom it is for, man, it's powerful. And it can be fast!

➤ RECOVERY

There are two aspects of the less traveled road I want to talk about here. The first one is recovery. A lot of what you're doing here—all of it in fact—is part of recovering from loss.

Traumatic, catastrophic loss is so devastating, so life changing, so brutal that there must be a recovery period. A time where you allow yourself to grieve, to experience and feel your feelings, to do the practical things that always need to be done.

In my case, I needed about fifteen months, but the first six months were where most of my actual recovery took place. The other nine months were the months that I did the "had-to's," like getting the house ready to sell; doing the yard sales, cleaning out the storage locker; settling the estate, moving, going through everything and shutting down my business. That's less recovery than clearing the way, I think, but recovery happened during that those activities as well.

During that time though, I had to give myself the space, the freedom, and the permission to recover. Part of the issue was that my guilt told me I deserved all of this pain and hurt. Talk about kicking me when I was down! But that's what devastating grief does.

When I was 18, I got jumped by five guys. It was an ambush. One minute I was walking down the street minding my own business, then next I heard *"There he is!"* The first punch knocked my glasses off and the second one knocked me to the ground, so all I could do was cover up while they beat and kicked me. They nearly beat me to death. I had to recover from that beating; and it took a while. That beating also changed me. It changed where I would go and what I would do there. I never saw those guys again. And I wasn't the "he" they were looking for. I was just in the wrong place at the wrong time with the wrong guys. It feels a lot like an analogy for my loss, now that I think about it.

But I fought recovery after that for a while, too. I've already detailed my struggle with getting stuck in the past, with being in my head, with being lost in grief. That was me refusing help.

I had to recover from all of that. I needed to be able to be open and curious again. I needed to see a future, and to take an active role in creating that future. I had to move forward. But I couldn't do any of that until I recovered.

Part of recovering is to begin the healing process. In the case of the beating, the bruises had to fade, the aches and pains had to go away, the loosened teeth needed to tighten back up and the cuts needed to heal. In the case of my loss, the wounds to my spirit and to my soul had to be treated; they had to able to close, to scab over and to become scars, not open wounds.

Really, recovery can be boiled down to a concept we've been talking about since the beginning of this book: understanding, owning, and accepting.

Recovery involves understanding not only what happened, meaning the loss and the circumstances leading up to it, but also understanding the place your loss has put you in.

This is uncharted territory. You're a stranger, in a strange land. This is not a journey you wanted to take; or one that you're prepared to take. You're helpless, hopeless, lost, and scared. You don't know what to expect. You have no idea what's going to happen next. You feel like you'll never get over it. You don't know if you *WANT* to get over it. And there's probably more.

This is *exactly* where I was after my loss. And I couldn't do anything from that place.

I had to recover first. You must recover too.

➤ RESTORATION

This book can be a part of your recovery process. You've learned some things. You've done some things. The biggest thing you've done though, is this:

You've set the table for restoration.

And that's the second part of the road less traveled.

I'm not going to spend a ton of time talking about restoration. Except to say this. Restoration is real. Restoration is what happens when your life is transformed after loss.

And it's outside of yourself. It's not something that you "do;" it doesn't have KPI's or Key Performance Indicators that you can adopt and execute in order to get it.

Simply put, restoration is manifestation. And to more closely define it, restoration actually means "more than before."

Most people misunderstand the word. They think it means to get back what they had before they lost it; to replace it. Homeowners insurance is bought with the "replacement value" not the "more than you had before value" . . . but that would be cool if it was! Although, people would probably be burning their homes down to get a better one, so maybe it's NOT such a good idea!

But restoration is *not* REPLACEMENT! It isn't about just getting back what you had.

Restoration is truly much better than that.

I know. Because I'm experiencing it in my own life.

I'm not going to tell you there's something you can do to experience restoration. I will say though, that I believe it's supernatural. It's mysterious. And it's cool.

I haven't talked about it a lot in here, but I believe that all of this—that transforming your life—is supernatural. It can't be explained. What I went through, what happened in my life, and what's happening now has no logical explanation.

So, I don't try to explain it or justify it. I just do what? I do what I've been asking you to do throughout these pages: I understand it the best I can. I own it. And I accept it.

Restoration is a Biblical principle. In the book of Job, he lost everything—to the point that his wife told him to basically go crawl into a hole somewhere and die. And that's what most people focus on. Job's losses. But they don't read the end of the book. The book of Job is 42 chapters. It's long. And it's a tough read. It's depressing. It's sad and it seems like it'll never end. It feels like loss and grief.

But at the end of the book, in the last seven verses of the forty-second chapter, something miraculous, something unexplainable and unexplained, happens. Job's fortunes are mysteriously restored.

What happened was that "the Lord gave Job twice as much as he had before."

Nowhere in the book is it explained as to how this happened; it just happened. Restoration happened.

So don't waste your time trying to understand the how's of restoration.

Instead, live in expectancy of it.

Believe in it.

Restoration is not something I can give you a blueprint for, like I have for the other things we've discussed here.

But when it comes to restoration, I can tell you this again: simply believe.

I believe.

And I believe for you.

Restoration is coming, my friend. A new day—a new life—is dawning.

A transformed life.

Let's move into the last two chapters and wrap this up, shall we?

Twelve

DECIDING WHAT YOU WANT

Oof! It feels like we've covered a lot. And that's true. We have. We're getting close to the end of the book now. But as I continue to say, the end of the book is the beginning of your personal transformation process.

We've covered a LOT of ground. And we're ready to close the loop, to come full circle.

So we're going to return to *Secret #1: Wanting & Willing.* You don't need to go back and re-read that chapter—unless you want to. This one, *Secret #12,* is one of the shortest chapters in the book.

It's time you decided what you want. What you *really* want.

You know what? On second thought, DO go back and review that chapter.

Or not. I'll let you decide. What do you WANT to do? Read it? Review it? Or not? Your call.

Then take it one step further.

Decide what you want, then be willing to have it. Write it down.

The best way to decide what you want is to get out of your head, and into your body. When you think about what it is that you want, about what you want your transformed life to be, how does it make your body feel?

Does your chest tighten up? Is your stomach tense? Are your back and shoulders knotted up?

Because if they are, your body is probably telling you that's not something you want. A tight stomach is usually associated with fear; knotted up shoulders and back muscles, generally with anger.

Unless that's what you want, try again.

If you want your transformed life to be happy, not negative; if you want your life to feel expansive instead of constricted or restricted—listen to your body.

This may sound "woo-woo;" it may sound out there.

I'm here to tell you it's not.

Remember when we talked about getting out of your head. There was a four-word phrase in my coaching advice to the client that I put in bold and italicized. That's because I really wanted you to see it. This is a phrase that Jason Su, one of my coaches, taught me and is constantly using.

"Feel more. Think less."

It's so important to understand and do this. I wear two bracelets. One says _"Never Quit"_ and the other says this: _"Feel More, Think Less."_ I need the reminders. Plus they're conversation starters sometimes when people ask me about them.

I put the words in bold, italicized them and even centered the phrase this time. I *really* want you to see this. To understand it. To own it, accept it and then do it. This one will change how you interact with yourself and with the world.

So, listen to your body. If your body feels good, your thoughts will be more expansive, brighter, bigger and bolder. More open and curious.

If your body tightens up, if it doesn't feel good, your thoughts will be more negative; more restrictive and contracted. Closed off.

Remember: Your thoughts are a reflection of what you're feeling physically.

Don't worry. You'll know the difference when you feel it. In fact, you already do.

When you experienced your loss, you were instantly thrown into a contracted, restrictive, negative state.

When you think of transforming your life, though, you get excited, you feel happy, maybe even a little nervous—(but it's a good nervous.) This is what thinking expansively feels like.

So, apply that to what you want. Finding what you want is a feeling. It's not a concept or something you have to wrap your mind around. You'll know it when you find it because it'll excite you. It'll light you up inside. So, find the excitement, find the light. **FEEL** it.

There's no judgment around what you want—there's simply wanting, then being willing to have it. One of the things about being willing to have it is that you don't need it; it's not tied to "needing" it. It's about wanting it.

Think less.

Feel more.

Find the excitement around what you want.

Feel the expansiveness.

There!! That's it!

Now write those things down.

There you are.

The Beginning. The End. The Discoveries. The Next Steps. (Truly) Deciding What You Want. There's your personal blueprint to *Transforming Your Life After Loss*.

That's it!

I'm going to disclose the final secret in the next chapter.

See you in there.

SECRET

Thirteen

The Ultimate Secret

It's *Always* Been Up to You

I'm going to ask that before you continue, please go back and do that.

Or not.

That's your decision. So, decide. Then act. One way or the other.

Your call.

Hey. Glad you made it. We are all the way through the book. This is the final chapter.

Of the book, that is. NOT the final chapter of anything else. In fact, this is where your *true* journey, your quest, your vision, your dreams . . . this is where all of that begins!

First, before I wrap it up, a story. I have a friend who's an absolutely amazing free-hand artist. He's a painter, and he does a lot of work in charcoal too. His name is Jeff Amano.

He started as a graphic novel illustrator, and now he and his wife, Claire, along with their English bulldog Maximillian (Max for short) travel around the country, living in their motorhome, and doing weekend shows. They set up a booth and Jeff draws and does paintings of people's dogs, done from photographs they give him.

He's fast. Somehow his brain is wired so that whatever he sees, either physically or in his head, he's able to render that onto a canvas or paper with lightning-fast speed, and accuracy.

His paintings and drawings ALWAYS look like his subjects. Always. He never misses.

I've had him do a couple for me.

But the one I really WANT him to do for me I'm still thinking about. I can see it in MY head. I'm not quite sure how to explain it to him so he can see it in HIS head. Because in order to get in onto a canvas in the way that it appears to me, he has to be able to see it the way that I see it.

And I'm not sure that'll ever happen. Because I CAN'T transfer a picture in my mind, or the one that's in my spirit, to him so he can see it in his.

And that's okay.

Because *I* can see it.

You know where I'm heading with this. It's in the title of the chapter. And it's the final secret.

Deciding what you want? Getting past this loss? Getting comfortable being uncomfortable? Discovering? Leaving the past behind and getting out of your head? Feeling more and thinking less? Understanding recovery and believing in restoration?

Transforming your life?

It's not about anybody else. It's ONLY about you. Period. Amen. 'Nuff said.

Let me tell you where I'm at right now. After writing this and going back and reading it and re-reading it again and again, I'm excited! I'm lit up inside! I'm smiling. I'm feeling quite satisfied. Because I know this work, this book, these steps, and techniques . . . I *KNOW*-that-I-know-that-I-know they work. They've worked for me.

But if I had tried to explain any of this to someone? If I'd tried to let them in my head so they could see what my transformed life is? If I'd tried to show them what I wanted? Before my life was transformed? What do you think would have happened?

A lot of things, and probably not very many of them good. They might have tried to talk me out of certain things. They might have poo-poo'd them. They might have made fun of me, or my ideas. They might have simply said, *"You'll never be able to do that."* Or some other soul-destroying words.

Here's where you may be right now. Where I HOPE you are in fact.

Meaning, I hope you're excited. I hope you're lit up. I hope you're as eager to transform your life as I was. I hope you know that in your hands, and now in your head, you've not only got the tools; you've also got the vision, the dream of what your transformed life is. You've got the power.

I said this was the last secret. Here's a bonus secret.

Be protective. Protect your dream, protect your vision. Don't talk about transforming your life. Just do it. Let your transformed life speak for itself.

I'm a poker player. In poker there's a concept called "cards speak." What that means, is that when you turn your hand over at showdown and it's the best hand, you win. You don't need to say a word. The cards speak for themselves. With transformation, as in poker, it doesn't matter what anybody else says. All that matters is what you have. Let it speak for itself. Let your "cards speak."

Adopt that principle with your life. Don't go around talking about what's going to be. Instead, just do the things. Do the work. Believe.

Then let your transformed life speak for itself. It will, you know. People will see it; they'll recognize it.

The 4th anniversary of my loss passed earlier this year. My sister sent me a text. It read, in part:

I . . . have been praying for you . . . I'm so very proud of you, for continuing to LIVE your LIFE and for spreading your joy to those around you! You are a most special man and I LOVE you!

A friend of mine, just this week, told me at church: "Man, I can't believe what's happened in your life in the last 4 years. It's God's grace!"

These were unsolicited comments. And they came, because these people saw what my life had become; what it's transformed into from where it was. And they saw what it was. They saw the ugliness, the tears; they heard the ranting and the raving.

I can tell you that after my loss, I certainly didn't see any of what my life has been transformed into coming. All I could see and feel, was death, darkness, and destruction. Of her. Of my life. Of me.

And somehow, somewhere that changed. It changed into focusing on and into pursuing light, life and love.

Because that's what life *should* be. It should be light, life and love.

Don't give someone else the power to destroy what you've

begun here. Hold it close, the beginnings of this transformed life of yours. Love it well. Take care of it and nurture it. Protect it.

It WILL happen, and then it will speak for itself.

I'll close the book with how I started this chapter:

I'm going to ask that before you continue, to please go back and do that.

Or not.

That's your decision. So, decide. Then act. One way or the other.

Your call.

Transforming your life? It's your call. It always has been. Now you have the tools to do it. Let me know how it goes. I'll see you there.

Much love.

CREATE A LIFE YOU LOVE

Thank you for reading my book. I hope you found it inspiring, uplifting, enlightening and motivational. But most of all, I hope you found it useful. I hope you're able to start using the concepts and tools you learned to begin transforming your life.

As you might imagine, this book is just the tip of the iceberg. It's an introduction to changing your life and creating the one you truly want. The one you love. Transformation *will* occur as you integrate what the book outlines into your life; it's impossible for it **NOT** to happen!

But it's not just about transformation.

Transformation is simply the beginning. The ultimate goal is to create a life you love. To get to a point where you can't wait to jump out of bed and say hello to every morning. I want you to create a life you're excited about and eager for.

A life that puts a constant smile on your face and song in

your heart. One that makes you look around with a big grin on your face and say out loud *"What does today have for me?"* And you get an answer you like!

Going deeper than simply transforming your life after loss means finding the ways to create that life.

As I continue to discover and marvel, it goes so much deeper. There's so much to look forward to! I know that I'll always be creating, living, and enjoying this life I love.

That realization causes so much joy to well up inside me! Knowing that I can keep transforming, keep getting better with restoration continuing to manifest in my life! To continue living this life that I truly love, every single day. One I never would have or could have imagined when I was dealing with all the loss and sadness.

It makes me so happy to realize that this journey of creating, discovering, transforming and restoration never has to end.

My journey has brought forth this book.

My desire to help others transform their own lives, and thereby create a life they'd truly love, has become both my destiny and my destination. This is what I was born to do.

If you feel as though this journey is also your destiny and you want it to become your destination, if you want to continue on to create the life you've always wanted, one you'd love, there are additional resources.

You can find them on my website at www.craftmethodcoaching.com. Check it out to learn more about who I am and what I'm up to.

As an email subscriber, you'll receive regular emails exploring and addressing more of how you can continue your own transformation process.

One of my "passion projects" is doing in-person workshops. This is where I get to take the book from words on a page and transform those into a living, breathing and dynamic process. To create an experience.

Because the workshops are shared experiences, they're a great place to discover new stuff. They're upbeat, they're fun and they're cool. They are also pressure-free. People don't get called out or called on. If someone wants to share something, we provide a safe space for that.

We also do a social meet-and-greet the evening before each workshop so people can get to know each other in a different setting. We have lunch together each day as well, so we can talk about what we're learning—or just talk.

It's always more fun to attend an event with a bunch of friends, and that's what happens with the workshop. People who go to the workshops make new connections they wouldn't have made anyplace else. Fellow attendees become friends.

We finish with our own spin on a wrap party. We don't call it that, though. We call it a "creation party." That's because we want to celebrate you, and what you're creating. It's important to be excited about that, to celebrate it and to enjoy it.

Coaching allows you to really go deep. The coaching model consists of a group of five to eight people and includes both group and individual coaching.

Podcast subscribers explore not only these topics but are also introduced to real people who have experienced real transformation. Ones who have created lives they love and who are doing so each day.

More books are coming. I've got talks to give and speeches to write and keynotes to build.

That's because creating a life you love, especially coming from one you didn't, is an ongoing process.

And it's an adventure!

If you'd like to explore the possibilities or continue the adventure, just let me know. We'll schedule an exploratory Roadmap call to see what's right for you.

Thanks for reading. I'll end this with how I always sign off.

I'm around. Let me know what you need. You can reach me in the following ways.

Text or call: (970) 596-0856

Email: john@craftmethodcoaching.com

Contact me through: www.craftmethodcoaching.com

Much love.

John

Acknowledgments

Nothing happens in a vacuum. And that includes the writing of *"Transforming Your Life After Loss: Finding Your Way to Peace, Joy & Happiness."*

I want to take a moment and say thank you to those who have helped me along the way.

First is my Lord and Savior Jesus Christ. Without His presence in my life, I simply wouldn't have survived what I went through nor would anything that came after ever have happened. There are many tangible reasons I trust Him with my life.

To that end, I have several spiritual mentors and guides that I follow for their take on things. Pastor Lawson Perdue, founder and lead pastor at Charis Christian Center in Colorado Springs is my pastor, a mentor, a guide but most of all, he's my friend. He's been there with me and for me through this entire journey. Thank you, Lawson. Find him and his ministry at www. charischristiancenter.com.

Others I want to thank are Jessie Duplantis, Joel Osteen and Kenneth Copeland. These full-gospel believers and teachers are instrumental to my mental.

Next is my family. My mother Pauline chose me when I was a baby. She and my dad, Dave, adopted me as an infant, and she's always been there for me through thick and thin. She's never judged me, but always supported me. I love you, Mom.

My sister DeAnn and my brother Rege have also always supported me in whatever I've done. They were there with me in my pain and have offered their thinking and advice when I needed it. Thank you both. I love you.

My son Jason and my daughter Katy went through this fire of loss with me on a daily basis. They were by my side from the beginning to the end of the tragedy of their mother's loss. They lost the one who was an absolute rock in their lives. They are warriors! They're strong and were my rocks for me when I just didn't have the strength.

My wife Tammy, who is part of my restoration. Meeting her was a God-thing and was divinely directed. I wouldn't be where I am without her wisdom, humor, honesty and her love. I love you, Tammy.

Two men, whom I've never met in person, but who I follow from afar, helped get me through some dark times. I mentioned in the beginning how I was inspired and reminded of who I was, and these are the two who did that for me.

The first is Marcus Luttrell, who is a Navy Seal and who you may recognize as the author of *"Lone Survivor"* (and movie of the same name) about Operation Redwings in Afghanistan, where he was the only survivor of a wartime mission gone very wrong.

He founded Team Never Quit, and through his website, I was both inspired to get out of being stuck; I re-discovered who I was, during one of the darkest periods of my life. Marcus reminded me of what the words and phrases "Never Quit" and "Never Out Of The Fight" really mean; and how to apply them to my life. His daily Facebook updates during the pandemic were hilarious too. I needed those laughs!

The second is Richie McPeak. I met him on the "Team Never Quit" Instagram page and started following and communicating with him.

Richie was not only a highly successful businessman with an outstanding line of supplements but he was also a cancer warrior. He understood loss about as well as anybody I've ever met. His personal battle, which he documented and shared publicly, and his, along with his family's response to what he dealt with, was nothing short of stunning. He and his family were, and remain, an inspiration to me, and to many others. His signature phrase was *"Every step is a finish line."* Sadly, we lost Ritchie earlier this year. But I know he'd say if he were still here, *"Keep going! Every step is a finish line!"* You can access his family's line of supplements at https://www.mcpeakmarket.com/.

As a coach, I have coaches. These are people who help me not only in staying focused, but who offer advice and assistance in getting done what I want to accomplish. Coaches always like to keep a professional distance from their clients, but I like to break that barrier down. That's why I don't call these two just coaches. I call them friends.

Blake Eastman is a high-level performance and poker coach to top-tier professional poker players and is also the founder of Beyond Tells and the Nonverbal Group, a behavioral research and education company. Blake is a former adjunct Professor of Psychology at City University New York (CUNY). He can be reached at www.nonverbalgroup.com.

Jason Su has been instrumental in me finding my way emotionally. He is a high-level performance coach whose style and techniques are transformative and life-changing. You can find him on X (formerly Twitter), LinkedIn, Instagram and on his website, www.pokerwithpresence.com.

It's critically important to have truth-tellers in your life; those who won't tell you only what you *want* to hear but will be fearless enough to tell you what you *must* hear. Both of these men are fearless. They have been, and remain, truth-tellers, in my life.

I can't say enough to or about either of them. Thank you both, Blake, and Jason.

To my website creator and designer, Colton Weidner. Colton is the founder and CEO of Done For You Technology. He caught my vision early on, and his ideas and creative thinking allow me to have the best possible website. One that clearly communicates what I want it to without being hard to navigate. Thanks, Colton. He can be reached at www.doneforyoutechnology.com and at colton@doneforyoutechnology.com.

His wife, Erin Bloom Davenport is an amazing Life Mastery coach who does one-of-a-kind retreats in Kenya, Africa and can be reached at www.lightofthetraveler.com.

To those who assisted me with the book itself.

First, many thanks to Emily Hugo, editor extraordinaire. Her input, corrections and advice make the book better and more readable. She helped me make the concepts and steps come across more clearly. Thanks, Emily

To Anna Paradox, who formatted the book. Thank you, Anna.

To Cliff Pelloni, published author, dad-chef and master facilitator of publishing and marketing. Cliff helped me see the book in a way I hadn't before and to realize it's much more than just a book. He's done so much from helping me create the best title and cover to all the other "behind the scenes" things, to the marketing, and much more. I'm really blessed to have been introduced to him. You can find Cliff at www.IdeatoAuthorPublishing.com.

These people are all rockstars!

And finally, thank *you*. Without you as a reader, there would be no reason for me to write, or to put words on a page.

I wish for you a life you've always wanted; a life *you* love.

Much love.

About the Author

At twenty-one, JOHN CRAFT stumbled upon Zig Ziglar's words: "Help enough other people get what they want and you will get what you want." This quote became the compass guiding John's life for over 40 years.

A decade-long period of personal and professional loss climaxed with the passing of his wife after a brief battle with cancer. From grief emerged a miraculous journey of recovery, leading John to create "Transforming Your Life After Loss: Finding Your Way to Peace, Joy & Happiness" and a new career as a transformational coach.

With a background in radio and entrepreneurship, John believes in a holistic approach to coaching, blending transformational and performance coaching with sales and business strategies.

Throughout his career, John has empowered countless individuals and small businesses, simplifying processes to help them realize their dreams and create fulfilling lives for themselves and their families.

John Craft, the founder of Craft Method Coaching, specializes in guiding those who've experienced significant loss toward recovery and restoration. His mission is to empower individuals to identify and live their dreams, freeing them from worry and fear to create lives they truly love.

You can find out more about John, his background and his work on his website located at www.craftmethodcoaching.com. He lives in Colorado.

Thank You Gift!!

I'm so glad you took this journey with me. As my gift for completing the book, I offer a free 30-minute Roadmap call to readers who wish to explore and get my feedback about their path forward.

This is not a sales call, but is exploratory in nature and is a $297 value.

You can book that with me through
www.craftmethodcoaching.com
on the Contact page.

www.ingramcontent.com/pod-product-compliance
Lightning Source LLC
Chambersburg PA
CBHW070831160726
48004CB00001B/334